THE POLI

BY CHRIS WELCH

Edited by Chris Charlesworth
Cover & Book designed by 4i,
Picture research by Nikki Russell

ISBN: 0.7119.5302.3 Order No. OP47800

Exclusive Distributors:
Book Sales Limited, 8/9 Frith Street, London W1V 5TZ, UK.
Music Sales Corporation, 257 Park Avenue South, New York, NY 10010, USA.
Music Sales Pty Limited, 120 Rothschild Avenue, Rosebery, NSW 2018, Australia.

To the Music Trade only:
Music Sales Limited, 8/9, Frith Street, London W1V 5TZ, UK.

Photo credits: Front and back cover; LFI: all other pictures
courtesy of LFI, Barry Plummer and Adrian Boot.

Printed in the United Kingdom by Ebenezer Baylis & Son, Worcester.

A catalogue record for this book is available from the British Library.

OMNIBUS PRESS
LONDON · NEW YORK · SYDNEY

CONTENTS

INTRODUCTION

Few could have predicted that out of the maelstrom of punk rock in the late Seventies would emerge two of the most powerful and successful sources of sophisticated music in pop history. The Police and Sting, their fountainhead, unleashed a flow of hit singles and albums that enriched the cultural world and enriched themselves beyond their wildest dreams.

The group transmuted the dross of punk energy into the gold of 'Reggatta de Blanc' a unique form of white reggae. They conquered the world while 'Sting' – Gordon Sumner – the humble milkman's son from Tyneside, became one of the wealthiest men in the land. As an actor, composer, lead singer with The Police, no mean bass player and owner of the most instantly recognisable vocal styles in pop, the very range of Sting's artistic achievements made him appear like a modern day Renaissance man.

The Police have long since broken up, but their influence has been enormous and their music and records remain an integral part of the fabric of rock. Together they recorded just five studio albums. Since 'going solo' Sting has released four studio and one double live CD.

The Police generally sustained a high standard, with only a few lapses in their output. In any case they created their own sound and truly distinctive style – that happy state few bands can ever hope to achieve. Sting's work since has reflected his love of jazz, blues and melody, and his lyrics have shone with a literate fluency, denied most workaday pop writers.

Problems and stress eventually blighted the career of The Police and led to its demise, but their greatest triumph lay in overcoming the crushing banality of the pop music system, and by dint of personality, forcing the acceptance of quality and originality – not always as easy as it might seem.

Neither The Police nor Sting fit comfortably into the pattern of normal rock development. Their backgrounds, experience, talents, intelligence and soaring ambition were far from run-of-the-mill. This sometimes made them a target for the jealous and suspicious. But for every bad review or scathing put-down, there was plenty of unstinting praise, admiration and encouragement.

Even music critics, castigated and consigned to Hades in the song 'St. Augustine In Hell' (from Sting's admirable 'Ten Summoner's Tales' album), found much to laud and applaud during the heyday of The Police and thereafter. Certainly in the early days when The Police, with their blond-haired, sharp-eyed lead singer, were the hottest, hippest property on the front pages, it seemed they could do no wrong. Everything they touched turned to gold.

The three young men who created The Police in 1977 did so at the height of the punk revolution, when upstarts with rings through their noses took delight in pouring scorn on the rock establishment, the old farts and dinosaurs whose millionaire lifestyles rankled young fans. If nothing else, punk created an environment where a new wave of young bands could snatch an early victory in terms of publicity and sales. The shake-up benefited even those musicians whose roots and musical ideals lay beyond the confines of angry 12-bar riffs and snotty lyrics.

The Police were formed by Stewart Armstrong Copeland, an experienced drummer fascinated by the rise of punk. Though now a resident of London, where he had drummed with Curved Air, he was an American citizen, whose father Miles was a jazz trumpet player who had played with the Glenn Miller Orchestra before he joined Army Intelligence during the Second World War and became a founding member of the CIA. The Copeland family have a fascinating history with complex connections in the world of big business and politics. When Stewart was only six months old his father was posted to Cairo, Egypt where he helped organise a secret intelligence service.

In 1956 he left the CIA and started his own agency, working mainly in the Middle East as an adviser to oil rich sheikhs. Stewart and his older brother, also called Miles, grew up in Beirut in the Lebanon and learned to speak fluent Arabic. Stewart began to play the drums at the age of 13, jamming in groups formed by young Americans living in Beirut. In 1966 Stewart's father moved to London and the boy was sent to Millfield public school. His older

brother, grandly known as Miles Axe Copeland III, managed various bands including Wishbone Ash and Curved Air and ran his own record labels. Later Stewart went to the University of California at Berkeley where he studied music, media and communications. In 1975 Miles asked his brother to be tour manager for Joan Armatrading, who was then signed to A&M Records. All this helped give Stewart considerable insight and expertise in the music business.

In the meantime Miles became involved with progressive rockers Darryl Way's Wolf. Violinist Darryl had been a member of Curved Air. After advising Darryl to fire his band, Miles took over as manager and set up a new group with Stewart and Darryl. This putative group was superseded by the need to reform the original Curved Air to pay off a tax liability. Stewart was retained as the band's tour manager, but after a tour, the drummer quit and Stewart finally took over the kit, backing singer Sonja Kristina. It was Stewart's first professional gig. However the pushy young drummer quickly saw that the band was wasting its money on expensively produced albums and he didn't like their commercial style. When the

band folded in December 1976, he already had plans for his own more up to date and aggressive group, The Police.

They began rehearsing in January and played their first gig in March. Stewart wanted a New Wave band which could take advantage of more realistic punk economics. He liked the idea that you could make your own records without major label interference. He recruited guitarist Henri Padovani and called a bass player and singer from Newcastle he'd had his eye on who called himself 'Sting.' Just a few phone calls was about to alter the course of rock history and all their lives.

Sting was born Gordon Matthew Sumner on October 2, 1951 in Wallsend, a district of Newcastle Upon Tyne. He was the eldest of four children from a Catholic family. His father was an engineer, who later worked as a milkman and eventually managed to set up his own dairy. Gordon's tense working class background instilled in him an early desire to break free of Newcastle and succeed in the music business. He was sent to St. Cuthbert's Grammar School which practised strict discipline and administered corporal punishment on a regular basis.

Gordon picked up the guitar while at school and after listening to The Beatles and Stones, was turned onto jazz by an older friend. After dropping out of Warwick University he took up playing bass guitar by night while holding down various day jobs, including labouring on building sites. Drifting somewhat aimlessly, in 1971 he decided to enrol at Newcastle Teachers' Training College, but his heart was more in jamming with jazz musicians at The Wheatsheaf, a local pub. Eventually he was invited to join The Phoenix Jazzmen and pepped up their acoustic sound with a powerful electric bass guitar. On stage he often wore a striped tee shirt that made him look like a bee, and the band's trombone player nicknamed him Sting – which stuck for evermore.

Sting completed his three year teacher's training course during which he gained experience teaching at a secondary school packed with beautiful schoolgirls. It was this period that led him to write 'Don't Stand So Close To Me', although he denied there was ever any impropriety between himself and his pupils. After graduating he took a job teaching at primary school in a mining village, while

he earned extra income playing jazz gigs. He rapidly became a local celebrity and joined the famed Newcastle Big Band. In 1974 he formed his own small jazz-rock group Last Exit. Sting began to write songs and sing, developing his own high-pitched vocal style, which he later said was influenced to a degree by jazz singer Cleo Laine.

In 1976 the Big Band split up and Sting married actress Frances Tomelty whom he had met while she was playing a Christmas show in Newcastle. Sting then decided to become a professional musician and give up his teaching job. He brought Last Exit to London and played several gigs, one of which at the LSE gained him his first mention in the music press, a review in *Melody Maker* by Karl Dallas. He also secured a publishing deal with Virgin Records, although they weren't interested in the band. The group returned to Newcastle, and by a twist of fate Stewart Copeland happened to be in town. He saw them play a gig at the Newcastle Polytechnic. He didn't like the band but he was very impressed with Sting. "He had a fantastic presence. It was pretty obvious he had enormous potential," said Stewart later. He spent a lot of time on the

phone trying to lure Sting back to London. Sting succumbed and brought down his wife and new-born baby to stay in a friend's cramped apartment.

The new group – Sting, Stewart and Henri – began rehearsing in Stewart's Mayfair flat. Said Sting: "Musically I thought Stewart's ideas were shit." Despite that, he was impressed by the fast talking American's energy. The idea was to play lots of short, snappy tunes and get down to the punk clubs where it was all happening. Although Henri was regarded as a somewhat limited guitarist, he played with the kind of feel the punk scene required.

Stewart and Sting both saw each other as ambitious, intelligent men who could probably achieve a lot together. There would be abrasive moments and many disagreements, but they knew they had to seize the time and make it work. Their first record 'Fall Out' was a brash, noisy punk opus, with Sting's voice raging above a busy bass riff, lots of crashing cymbals and guitar licks closer to The Who than The Sex Pistols. They injected the same kind of raw energy into songs like 'Nothing Achieving' and 'Dead End Job.' Recalled Sting later: "'Fall Out' was one of the first songs Stewart played

me. What they lacked in sophistication they made up for in energy. I just went along with them and sang them as hard as I could." Sting particularly liked the fast moving 'Dead End Job' which was recorded by the band later with Andy Summers.

The band denied they were 'false punks'. They played with just as much fire and anger as other bands on the scene, and when Sting shouted out songs like 'Landlord' he sang from the heart. He and Frances had just been thrown out of the house they were renting.

The Police paid for the recording and pressing of 'Fall Out' themselves and had 2,000 copies pressed for sale on their own Illegal Records label. They also went out on the road supporting American punk singer Cherry Vanilla which gained them press attention and gave them touring experience. It was the beginning of a hectic period of hard touring, without money or recognition, during the Spring of 1977. But 'Fall Out' sold out its first pressing and later went on to sell 100,000 copies.

In June Andy Summers went to see The Police playing at The Marquee. He'd already jammed with Sting and Stewart in a one-off band called Strontium 90, the result of a Gong reunion show in Paris. He was impressed with the band and was desperate to join. For a while The Police became a four piece, retaining Henri Padovani on guitar but he was unable to play the new songs that Sting was writing. The band wanted a guitarist who could keep the punk energy but play with more technique and a more adventurous style. Eventually the new recruit took over the lead role and The Police became a three piece once more.

Andy Summers was born Andrew James Somers on December 31, 1942, in Poulton-le-Fylde, Lancashire. Later the family moved to Bournemouth where Andy specialised in music at school. At the age of 17 he was spotted by Bournemouth-born band leader and organist Zoot Money, and he joined Zoot's legendary Big Roll Band, one of the finest R&B groups of the Sixties, who played regularly at London's Flamingo Club. Later Andy joined Zoot in the newly formed Dantalion's Chariot, a brave attempt to latch onto the hippie movement.

He later played with Eric Burdon's New Animals and went to live in the States for six years where he studied classical guitar. Then he moved with his second wife Kate back to London, changing his name to Summers and

playing with the Kevin Coyne band and on projects like Mike Oldfield's 'Tubular Bells.' When Oldfield's show reached Newcastle he met Sting whose Last Exit was the support act. In 1976 he joined the Kevin Ayers band but when he encountered Sting and Stewart Copeland again, he knew he was destined to be part of The Police.

Sting, Stewart and Andy played their first gig at Rebecca's, Birmingham, on August 18. By now they had already hit upon mixing reggae with rock rhythms and making extensive use of Andy's echo effects on the guitar. During a trip to Europe, they ended up in Paris, where Sting saw prostitutes at work in the red light district and was inspired to write 'Roxanne'. In December they started work on their first album 'Outlandos d'Amour' which they paid for themselves.

The final ingredient which would help seal their success and solidify the image came when Sting and Andy were obliged to dye their hair blond for a Wrigley's Chewing Gum TV commercial. Stewart already had blond hair, and the combined effect of similar hairstyles and colour was to make them appear as brothers. Observers with long memories weren't slow to note that the last band to capitalise on similar hairstyles came from Liverpool and revolutionised the pop industry.

Early in 1978 Miles Copeland, their manager, obtained a deal to release 'Roxanne' as a single, but it failed to chart as the group was in Germany and unavailable to promote it in the UK. Their next single 'Can't Stand Losing You' got into the Top Fifty however, and in October they set off on their first American tour and made their début at CBGB's in New York. 'Outlandos d'Amour' was released in November and the album shot to Number 6 in the UK charts.

The Police were on their way, and from subterranean rumblings and underground rumours, they suddenly burst on the public in a wave of air play and publicity. Sting was further catapulted to national fame by his appearance as a Mod - Ace The Face - in The Who's film *Quadrophenia*. Events came in a rush. 'Roxanne' was re-issued and leapt up the charts, and after their first UK tour in February 1979 they began work on their second album 'Reggatta de Blanc' which included the blockbuster hits 'Message In A Bottle' and 'Walking On The Moon'.

The combination of Sting's high pitched, anguished vocals, Andy's spatial guitar and Stewart's busy, tricky drumming, together with a flow of imaginative, atmospheric songs, proved irresistible. From then on the band dominated the charts, endlessly toured the world, and watched the gold and platinum albums and singles pile up with the luggage. At the same time, under Miles Copeland's astute management, The Police also racked up far higher earnings than any of their contemporaries.

After the albums 'Zenyatta Mondatta', 'Ghost In The Machine' and 'Synchronicity' The Police were physically, mentally and perhaps creatively exhausted. During 1984 they were expected to release a 'live' album, but it never appeared. By 1985 they had effectively broken up and attempts to record a new album together were abandoned.

Sting launched his solo career with 'The Dream Of The Blue Turtles' in June 1985, and sang without his old group at Live Aid on July 13. In the aftermath of The Police, Andy Summers recorded his own albums with Robert Fripp, while Stewart Copeland began a new career writing film music and even composing an opera.

On June 11, 1986, the Police reunited to perform five songs at an Amnesty International show in Atlanta, Georgia as part of the Conspiracy Of Hope tour which also included U2 and Peter Gabriel. It would be their last public appearance together. In July 1986 the band went to a London studio with the idea of recording what would have been their sixth album, but because of constant arguments between Sting and Stewart they managed to produce only one track, a re-make of 'Don't Stand So Close To Me', which took them three weeks to record. Andy Summers later described the sessions as "absolutely torturous." It seemed clear to Andy and Stewart that Sting had no intention of writing any new songs for the band. The torture would soon be over, as the band went their separate ways.

While Andy and Stewart both embarked on suitably satisfying personal projects, it was obvious that their ex-singer would enjoy the most visible success. It wasn't long before he recruited a superb all-American jazz-rock group to back him on his tours and albums and he was free to develop his musical ideas without acrimony or in-fighting. Over the next decade he would enjoy enormous success,

although his personal popularity took a mid-term dive when he appeared to be taking himself rather too seriously.

Sting used his wealth and free time to devote himself to important world causes which sometimes led to accusations of pomposity. He was obliged to assure commentators he was at heart an ordinary man, who simply cared about what he saw on TV news and felt he should take some action. And he did – in the end – save some of the Brazilian rain forest, one of his chief concerns. His music became rather too tortured for comfort in mid-life, epitomised by the gloomy introspection of his album 'Soul Cages' (1991). But by the release of 'Ten Summoner's Tales' (1993) the humour, warmth and spirit that was always an essential part of his work returned.

Throughout his career with The Police and with his own bands, Gordon Sumner has always sought to appeal to the intelligence of his audience, rather than insult them. It's one thing to be blessed with talent. It's another to find the courage to put it to the test. All three bared their souls and that was the ultimate triumph of The Police... and of Sting.

CHRIS WELCH,
West Wickham, Kent, 1995

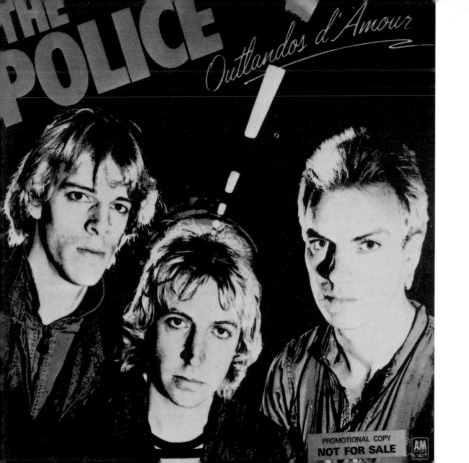

THE POLICE

Outlandos d'Amour

A&M

OUTLANDOS D'AMOUR

(ORIGINAL UK ISSUE: A&M AMLH 68502, RELEASED OCTOBER 1978; CD A&M CDA 68502,
RELEASED MARCH 1989; CDMID 126, RELEASED AUGUST 1991)

A trio of blondes fixed the public with a penetrating gaze as they stared out from the cover of the most eagerly awaited début of the late Seventies. Here was the album that would point the way to an exciting new decade, an era of sharp new sounds, bold new voices and a period of expansion and boom. Although The Police were born of the anarchic indie punk movement, their attitude was perfectly suited to the impending age of Thatcherism and Reaganomics. Not that Sting, as poet and humanitarian would agree with such a stark analysis, but certainly the huge success of The Police, their pursuit of world domination and the businesslike clarity of their approach seemed in tune with the keenly competitive Eighties. Indeed some early critics of The Police would complain that their music was harsh and cold. Gone was the laid back, muffled and soporific sound of so much Seventies rock.

Those were the days when nasal singers warbled of life 'on the road', while the drums and guitars were swathed in sticky tape and blankets by engineers with cotton wool in their ears. 'Outlandos d'Amour' was a celebration of ambition and freedom, infused with a startling sense of purpose and drive. Sting's collection of sharply drawn songs, epitomised by 'Can't Stand Losing You', were clever and witty, and the band's daring blend of reggae with punk caused a sensation. The album was recorded at Surrey Sound Studios, and produced by the band with the assistance of engineers Nigel and Chris Gray.

Work began in January 1978 and Sting wrote several tracks, one of which he regarded as merely 'a throwaway'. This turned out to be 'Roxanne' the band's first major hit that eventually transformed their fortunes. Recalled Sting: "I didn't think much more about it, until we played the album to Miles Copeland. When we got to 'Roxanne' we were a bit embarrassed because the song was an anachronism. Compared with our usual material it was slow, quiet and melodic." Instead of dismissing the song, Copeland announced that it was "amazing". Sting was thrilled and Miles was so impressed he took the track to A&M who agreed to release it as a single, leading to a full record contract.

But there was little or no airplay. Despite rave reviews in the music press, the BBC refused to play a song which seemed to be about a love affair with a prostitute. It wasn't until the single took off in America that 'Roxanne' charted in England, dragging 'Outlandos d'Amour' with it. "I felt very strongly about 'Roxanne' because that was a serious song about a real relationship," said Sting. "It wasn't a smutty song in any sense of the word."

The song was born out of the trip to Paris in October 1977. The band played a gig which turned out to be a disaster, as nobody turned up to see them or headliner Wayne County. Sting took a walk through the city's red light district and was captivated by the sight of beautiful Parisian prostitutes on parade. He imagined what it would be like to fall in love with one of the girls. Sting also fell in love with the name. Roxanne was apparently Alexander the Great's wife and also Cyrano De Bergerac's girlfriend!

NEXT TO YOU

Punk roots show through on this exuberant pogo-ing rocker, redolent of safety pins and Vortex Club violence. Stewart Copeland's drums, although still sounding strangely flat at this time, push the beat with a brisk energy. At least you can hear it's a real drum kit – there was no 'sampling' in '78. Sting whoops with joy at Andy Summer's sliding guitar solo, and snaps out the age old lover's quandary: "What can I do... all I want is to be next to you!" Short, breathlessly simple, and a spirited way to introduce a brash new group to a tough world waiting to be impressed.

SO LONELY

Reggatta De Blanc – white reggae – makes its first appearance, and Sting assured the critics that he had no problem with absorbing the all-pervasive reggae influence. After all, England had been in the front line of West Indian music trends since the late Fifties, from Calypso and Bluebeat right up to roots reggae. Anyway it was nice to know that Bob Marley liked The Police. Sting later confirmed that the band were 'total Bob Marley fans' and claimed that during the nihilistic punk era, reggae was the only enjoyable alternative. The tune has some slight resemblance to 'No Woman No Cry', utilising the chords of C, G, A Minor and F. Sting nurses his broken heart in lonely solitude, in high pitched, strangled tones that threaten to damage his vocal cords. However, the strain of singing in such a high register adds to the poignancy of his vocal delivery. The unexpected changes in tempo and the quirky nature of Andy's guitar work, a mixture of howling rock and off the wall country licks, defines the sound of a band at the cutting edge. Sting's screaming and his own backing vocals drive towards a manic climax.

ROXANNE

The sound of one of the mightiest hits of the decade is ushered in by laughter. "Roxanne – you don't have to put on the red light," chuckles Sting in his best Jamaican accent. "Those days are over. You don't have to sell your body to the night." Sting later denied that 'Roxanne' was a reggae song. "It's actually a tango! But going from that relaxed lope into full rock'n'roll really appealed to me."

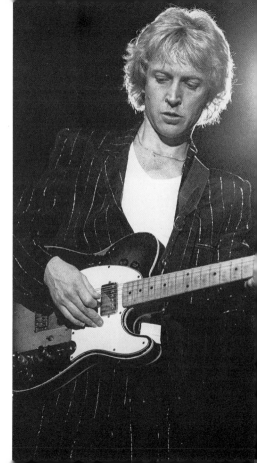

The clipped guitar pulse over the upside down, back to front drum and bass rhythms gripped the public's imagination, once radio allowed them a chance to hear it. 'Roxanne' became an underground hit with the band's fans, long before it reached the charts. An especially intriguing aspect of this crucial song is its simplicity, brevity, and daring use of complete silence. Vaguely inconclusive, like so many Police performances, the push me, pull you rhythmic sense sustains its hypnotic appeal, while Sting emotes all manner of messages, thoughts and emotions into a world-weary cry for love.

HOLE IN MY LIFE

'There's a hole in my life,' reveals Sting in a piece that serves as a counterpoint to the mood already established by 'Roxanne.' Stewart sets up a back beat based on what is known as a 'flam', two beats played almost together thus, 'fa-lam!' Andy sets up a one-note riff that pervades a spare, spartan but tense vehicle for one of Sting's least affected performances. The chorus has a Beatle-ish swelling grandeur, but it tends to go on rather too long for comfort and suffers from a messy ending.

PEANUTS

Copeland gets busy and Sting gets in a few clipped and hurried phrases, before Andy launches into an extraordinary solo, full of unexpected twists. His anger matches Sting's protestations about not wanting 'to read about a lifelong friend', doubtless in some newspaper exposé that is part of the price of fame. The madness increases as an erratic soprano sax is brought into play and Sting briefly quotes from the old 'Peanut Vendor' jazz standard.

CAN'T STAND LOSING YOU

Another of the band's early excursions into reggae, although the main thrust is contrasted with moments of hard rock vigour. Sting's lyrics deal with the perils of a tempestuous affair in which his precious LPs "are all smashed", adding for good measure: "you'll be sorry when I'm dead and all this guilt will be on your head," a threatened suicide note that caused some consternation in the corridors of rock power. Once again the BBC wireless telegraphy service was none too happy about broadcasting its rhythmic message to the nation, and a tasteless picture of a hanged man on the single sleeve probably didn't assist the band's case. But then, you know - these guys.

TRUTH HITS EVERYBODY

Despite the hubbub of this rapid fire rocker, key phrases leap out of the mix, like Sting's "I stepped outside of myself and felt so cold." Bells toll mysteriously over the rhythm guitar riff and there is a strong Who influence about some of the open chords. The drive however is all Police, and the engineers have fun with a thunderous climax.

BORN IN THE 50's

Not much to celebrate here, with a rather banal hook line, but it seems that way now probably due to a surfeit of Fifties nostalgia songs. This has deeper roots as Sting croaks and bawls about the generation who grew up in the shadow of The Bomb. But despite the social comment it sounds like something Bruce Springsteen would gargle in his bathroom.

BE MY GIRL-SALLY

A comic music hall style episode as Andy Summers tells the tale of Sally, an inflatable doll that becomes his wife. Very droll.

MASOKO TANGA

After the above ill-advised comic interlude, the album gets back on track, with a rock steady work-out that features some fine bass playing, nifty hi-hat work, bongos, congas and backward tapes intercut with some of Andy's coolest jazz grooves. Sting's shameless scat singing is very effective. This is a band jamming with absolutely no regard for commercial strictures. No producer today would allow such freedom – or such a surreal finale. This undulating performance underlines the division between a band's need to express itself and its role as a back up team. Any guitar rock band attempting this today would be shown the studio door and immediately replaced by samplers, tape loops, drum machines and plastic cups of coffee.

THE POLICE

Reggatta de Blanc

A&M

REGGATTA DE BLANC

(ORIGINAL UK ISSUE: A&M AMLH 64792, RELEASED SEPTEMBER 1979; CD A&M CDA 64792, RELEASED SEPTEMBER 1989; CD A&M CDMID 127, OCTOBER 1992)

By the time the world was catching up with 'Roxanne' and 'Outlandos d'Amour' The Police were well into their stride with their blockbusting second album, which entirely lived up to expectations and took the band to new heights of success and popularity. Sting surpassed himself with brilliant new songs, including the hugely inventive and infectious 'Message In A Bottle' and 'Walking On The Moon', one of the most atmospheric songs known to science – even if the moon doesn't have an atmosphere. Who needs oxygen when Sting breathes such life into the pop biosphere!

The band began work on 'Reggatta de Blanc' in February 1979. Technically, the sound was much improved on the 'Outlandos' sessions. Engineer Nigel Gray transformed the Surrey Sound studios by upgrading them from 16-track to 24-track and the band could afford to buy £6,000 worth of studio time, which translated into four weeks spread over several months. At first however, the sessions seemed much harder work than on the previous album. They had fewer songs finished, although Sting was ready to contribute three blockbusters, including 'The Bed's Too Big Without You'. Stewart and Sting had to combine forces to come up with material like 'It's Alright For You' in an effort to pad out the album. The sessions were interrupted by another American tour in April 1979, during which time The Police suddenly hit the jackpot and 'arrived' as 'Roxanne' and 'Outlandos' began their climb up the charts. When 'Reggatta de Blanc' was released it rocketed to Number One in the UK charts where it stayed for four weeks in October 1979. It became *de rigueur* to own a copy of the album with its distinctive blue and silver cover.

MESSAGE IN A BOTTLE

Here was a simple enough concept, but as any songwriter might bemoan "Why didn't I think of that?" The band rise magnificently to the occasion, playing with a cohesion and confidence not always apparent on the first album. Sting drops some of his rough edged mannerisms, while retaining the Marley influence. Compared with the original vinyl release, his voice appears lower pitched on the CD version, an effect probably due to the vagaries of turntable speeds. The bass and guitar swirl in a kind of rotary action while Sting sets up the theme. Then the band rocket into overdrive, all part of their amazing ability to turn a live rock performance into a hit. Strange that actor Sting should pronounce the line "Sending out a Nesso Ess", and not "an S.O.S." Diction, dear boy, diction. Sting explains that 'Message' is a song about loneliness and alienation. "It's about finding solace and other people going through the same thing. The guy's on a desert island and he throws a bottle out to sea saying he's alone and these millions of bottles come back saying 'So what? So am I!'" 'Message In A Bottle' became the band's first Number One hit.

REGGATTA de BLANC

White reggae, unlike white bread, has considerable taste and fibre, at least from the evidence of these layers of rhythm, untrammelled by too many lyrics. Here is a chance to just lay back and enjoy the Summers/Copeland axis hit a groove. Stewart uses the butt end of his stick on the snare drum with all the rapid fire of a latter day Art Blakey.

This was an instrumental the band had been featuring in its 'live' set before the album was mooted.

IT'S ALRIGHT FOR YOU

When The Police were 'up' and feeling punky, they locked into a piece that speaks volumes about their combined musical experiences. You can hear a touch of Dylan in Sting's shouting, declaiming delivery, larded by a spot of Johnny Rotten. But what bilge we critics speak, when descending into the unprofitable world of comparisons. This is Sting, Andy and Stewart jamming and enjoying life before it all became too complicated.

BRING ON THE NIGHT

A blending of soprano and tenor vocals achieved by the miracle of double tracking. Andy holds down a long note before the rhythm

section claps on more sail. All manner of subtleties go on as Stewart taps out a spartan bass drum rhythm. It doesn't lead anywhere in particular but it's ideal smoking material.

DEATHWISH

The drums kick off with a Bo Diddley beat, as Andy's guitar sets up an echoing cascade of chords on a piece that marks time rather than expands the frontiers of our knowledge. "Burning in the outside lane – people think that I'm insane," chants Sting contemplating the lack of courtesy on the road. Useful film music perhaps but not one of the band's most meaningful works.

WALKING ON THE MOON

Brilliance and perfection achieved on one magical performance. One of the most memorable introductions ever committed to magnetic tape – a simple bass line and the dancing, skipping hi-hat – launches Sting into vocal orbit. It had already been ten years since the first Moon landings, but this song seemed to perfectly encapsulate both the residual awe at the conquest of space and the light giddiness induced by the conquest of sex, love and rock'n'roll. The band keep the sound as sparse as possible. Commented Sting: "As a three piece what was intelligent about us was, instead of trying to pretend we were a bigger band, we used that limitation to our advantage. There were some big black holes in 'Walking On The Moon' and that guitar chord Andy came up with was just mind-blowing." The single was a Number One hit in the UK in December 1979.

ON ANY OTHER DAY

No wonder there was such reported antipathy between Sting and Stewart Copeland over the band's material. If this was the best that Stewart could do, then Sting was entitled to be irritated. The best that can be said is that the humour of the piece serves to contrast with the ethereal mood established by 'Walking On The Moon'. But it makes you ponder why anyone would insist on including this absurdity on such an important, classic album. Stewart ill-advisedly breaks into song then warns "The other one's a complete bullshit".

THE BED'S TOO BIG WITHOUT YOU

Stewart redeems himself with his superb snare drumming behind Sting's wandering bass line, on the album's third greatest hit. A simple phrase, a neat concept.

CONTACT

More disasters – another Copeland special that should have been relegated to the editing suite floor. Instrumentally fine of course, with tempo changes, a doomy bass line and clipped, precise drumming. But the lyrics don't make it and the tune is a makeshift filler.

DOES EVERYONE STARE

Yet *another* Stewart Copeland song! Now he mentions it – Stewart does tend to fix people with a rather amused and intense glare. Built over a piano riff and with a touch of the Lotte Lenya's, this Germanic cabaret stuff has no place on a Police record. It completely unbalances the whole thrust of the band's direction and concept. Maybe Stewart should have cut his own ten inch album.

NO TIME THIS TIME

After a huge chunk of unprofitable activity on the second side of the original album, The Police get back on track with this fast moving, exciting piece on which Stewart does what he does best – play magnificent drums, complete with four-bar breaks in the final hectic moments. Live rock!

ZENYATTA MONDATTA

(ORIGINAL UK RELEASE: A&M AMLH 64831, OCTOBER 1980; CD A&M CDA 64831, SEPTEMBER 1986; CD A&M CDMID 128, OCTOBER 1992)

The Police's third album saw the band maturing in both its musical approach and lyrical content – even if it contained the world's most immature song title: 'De Do Do Do, De Da Da Da!' However Sting, who wrote the majority of the material, had a reason behind this seeming plunge into banality. As he explained: "'De Do Do Do' was an articulate song about being inarticulate. Anyway it was a huge hit on both sides of the Atlantic."

Sting wrote the lyrics as an experiment in pop innocence, taking his cue from such past classics of simplicity as 'Da Do Ron Ron' by The Ronettes and 'Doo Wah Diddy' by Manfred Mann. "They weren't trying to tell you anything or distort your vision," he said. "It was just sound. In the song I try to intellectualise and analyse why that works so effectively." By now the band had long eschewed any lingering vestiges of punk. Said Sting: "We felt we could dismiss this idea that we'd been punks and we could make music we really wanted to make."

'Zenyatta Mondatta' was recorded at Wisseloord Studios in Hilversum, Holland, mainly for tax reasons, and was produced by the band with engineer Nigel Gray. It would turn out to be Nigel's last album with the band, following a disagreement with manager Miles Copeland.

The band had been engulfed in a gruelling world tour that had included trips to India and Egypt. The epic journey began in January 1980 and would visit 37 cities and 19 countries, possibly the biggest rock tour ever devised. The last date of the tour was at Sting's home town of Newcastle where 40,000 people applied for just 4,000 tickets.

During all this hard work, there had been little time for song writing and since 'Reggatta de Blanc' Sting had come up with only one number, 'Driven To Tears'. The band took a two month break and Sting escaped to a new home in Galway, Ireland, to work on the album. He adopted a new approach, realising that the songs on previous albums like 'Outlandos d'Amour' had tended to be rather self centred. "The songs on 'Outlandos' were all me, me, me," he said. "With 'Zenyatta' I turned to what's happening outside. I hadn't seen the world for a start. And I was too interested in me."

However, once the sessions started it became clear there were problems. The band felt tired and uninspired and it was hard work to get motivated and to finish the album on time. Stewart Copeland later revealed: "We had bitten off more than we could chew. We finished the album at 4 am on the day we were starting our next world tour."

Despite the pressure, or perhaps because of it, the band created some superb new music, and the album went straight to Number One in the UK charts in Autumn 1980 and stayed there for four weeks, alongside a Number One Hit single, 'Don't Stand So Close To Me'. In America the album stayed in the Top 20 for six months, peaking at Number 5 and achieving Platinum status with a million sales.

DON'T STAND SO CLOSE TO ME

An ominous drone ushers in one of Sting's last great contributions to The Police canon of songs. It's a brilliant concept, a song of temptation and frustration about the teacher and his pet pupil – Lolita in a gym slip. In fact Sting mentions Vladimir Nabakov, the Russian-born American author of the controversial book about the forbidden love of an intellectual for a 12-year-old girl. It was Nabakov who coined the phrase 'nymphet'. Never was a dire warning more passionately delivered as Sting chronicles the developing human disaster as "the accusations fly".

Although Sting had worked as a school teacher early in his career, he emphatically denied that he ever had any such relationships with his pupils - nor ever wanted to. The song developed more out of the band's perceived effect on young girl fans at the height of their fame. The rest of the band – all two of them – respond magnificently, and the single sold a million copies in the UK alone and was a Top Ten hit in the States in April 1981.

DRIVEN TO TEARS

An expression of rage against the spectacle of starving children in the Third World, brought to the West by the technology of television. We can afford the technology but not the food. Sting wrote this during a US trip a couple of years earlier. It surges with an unstoppable anger.

WHEN THE WORLD IS RUNNING DOWN, YOU MAKE THE BEST OF WHAT'S STILL AROUND

Here is an example of The Police rhythm section at its best, going with the flow and just grooving with apparent ease. It's all the skill born of long practise. Sting shows an early appreciation of the outside world in his lyrics that go beyond mere concerns of the flesh.

CANARY IN A COALMINE

A lively, fun track with an irresistible guitar flutter and a quite charming theme matched by Sting's wryly observant lyrics. He tells the

POLICE : ZENYATTA MONDATTA

object of his affections that she leads her life like the aforementioned canary, getting so dizzy that walking in a straight line proves difficult. Curious analogy but perhaps Sting was recalling life in the coal pits of his native North East.

VOICES INSIDE MY HEAD

A distant Sting sings in relaxed fashion as the axis of Summers and Copeland jam in time honoured Police fashion, playing one of those grooves that could go on for hours in the studio without anyone losing interest. Stewart plays some of those nippy fills that inspired a generation of drummers, delighted all producers and engineers and probably went straight over the heads of most of the broad masses.

BOMBS AWAY

Stewart returns to the writer's role and at least makes up for past blunders with a strongly worded assault on macho warlords. "The General scratches his belly and thinks, his pay is good but his officers stink… The President looks in the mirror and speaks, his shirts are clean but his

country reeks." Presumably the band weren't planning on a tour of the world's major trouble spots. Andy gets a chance to go native on the guitar, while Third World types chant in their usual heathen manner. A vast improvement on Stewart's 'Reggatta' contributions.

DE DO DO DO, DE DA DA DA

Another classic intro – as Andy and Stewart accent the positive aspects of this otherwise simple but hugely appealing ditty that went Top Ten in the States, their first big hit there since 'Roxanne'. It stayed in the US *Billboard* chart for 13 weeks, from its entry in November 1980. In the UK the single went to Number 5 in December. Sting cheerfully explains that the meaningless phrase is all that a lover sometimes wants to say to his babe, to cast aside the fine words of the poets and revel in lost innocence. Not a bad ruse at that.

BEHIND MY CAMEL

Summers decides to fight back against the dominance of Sumner and his many tales, and

contributes this mysterious guitar theme which won a Grammy Award for best instrumental rock performance of the year, following in the footsteps of 'Reggatta de Blanc'. But it wasn't really the best. Andy could have done much better.

MAN IN A SUITCASE

Ambient noise of announcements as Sting grumbles at life living in a suitcase. "Must I be a man with a stranger's face?" he demands. It's doubtless aimed at the band's agent, busy booking gigs from Cairo to Newcastle via Neasden.

SHADOWS IN THE RAIN

A return to reggae and padded out with some plinking piano notes, obviously not supplied by Oscar Peterson. Andy seems to be having a fit in a room some way down the corridor. Signs of road fever and paranoia? A track fit only for the studio bin, along with empty beer bottles and sundry cheeseburger wrappers.

THE OTHER WAY OF STOPPING

And so ends a generally satisfying album apart from the odd aberration like 'Shadows', and this indulgent jam, another contribution from 'S. Copeland'. Who knows what pressures the band were under in the studio that made them produce this instead of another blockbuster that would satisfy fans, their manager, the engineer and the tea boy? If they couldn't always find a seam of gold, then it only emphasised the essential frailty of the creative. When The Police were hot, they were astounding. When the spark of genius failed to ignite, they were merely human.

THE POLICE

GHOST IN THE MACHINE

GHOST IN THE MACHINE

(ORIGINAL UK RELEASE: A&M AMLK 63730, OCTOBER 1981;
CD A&M CDA 63730 1983; CD A&M CDMID 162, OCTOBER 1992)

As the Techno Eighties dawned, micro processors and computers began to enter every household, and business and scientific progress seemed to be accelerating at alarming speed. The music industry was among the first to take advantage of the new technology. The sound of Police albums and singles were highly advanced compared to the flat and uneven rock recordings of preceding years. Perhaps inspired by these changes, and the growing dominance of computers and scientific rationality, Sting pondered on magic, other worlds and the spiritual side of man's psyche. He felt the range of human senses was being blunted or distorted by electronic interference. Paradoxically there was something magical in the blending of human thought and jumping electrons.

Perhaps there was a ghostly presence in the new machines, lurking amidst the circuits and behind the flickering screens. In his musings, Sting had been influenced by the writings of philosopher Arthur Koestler. The title 'Ghost In The Machine' referred to the human spirit in music, expressed through the technological facilities of a recording studio. These ideas would permeate the band's fourth album.

As The Police embarked on 'Ghost' they had reached a pinnacle of achievement in the material world. Their records sold in millions. As they toured the world, they were acclaimed in myriad countries and greeted as idols. It all resulted in considerable personal pressure and it was not always easy to find inspiration for new songs. They had been away from the studios for a considerable time before Sting got around to writing once more. He'd also been busy with film and TV work, as well as touring with The Police. Finally, on June 15, 1981, they set off for Montserrat in the Caribbean, to start work at AIR, the famed studio, set up by The Beatles' producer, George Martin.

For the first time since 'Outlandos d'Amour' they had a new producer/engineer.

With Nigel Gray no longer involved, they were introduced to Hugh Padgham, famed for his work with Genesis and Phil Collins. Padgham had just finished work on Collins' break through 'Face Value' album and was a firm believer in the big, sharp drum sound. This had been pioneered by Phil and Peter Gabriel, who swept away the old muffled sound of the Seventies. Padgham was recommended to The Police by XTC's Andy Partridge. While it was intended to retain The Police 'sound', the material is less neurotic than on 'Zenyatta Mondatta'. The band's instrumental range was enhanced by the use of keyboards, and layers of saxophone riffs added by Sting, who had recently had lessons.

'Ghost In The Machine', despite the inclusion of a few sub-standard tracks, easily topped the UK album charts and in the States remained at Number Two for some six weeks. In the wake of this album, the band played fewer gigs and for a while it seemed the group had split up, to rest, contemplate their individual futures and explore their inner selves.

SPIRITS IN THE MATERIAL WORLD

'Are there spirits in the material world?' Sting was attacked for being 'pretentious' for daring to admit he had read a few books, in this case by philosophers Arthur Koestler and Carl Jung. Their influence imbues this ghostly example of musical alchemy and Sting's lyrical explorations.

EVERY LITTLE THING SHE DOES IS MAGIC

Stewart's clipped hi-hat and stick rhythms set up a sultry mood before a dying swan of a bass note heralds a launch into more feverish activity. It's an irresistible ditty once Sting gets into his stride, but there are ceaseless course corrections and intriguing twists. The spartan core sound is embellished with rhapsodic piano interjections from Jean Roussel. This superb love song became a Number One hit in the UK in October 1981, and went to Number Three in the US *Billboard* Top 40.

INVISIBLE SUN

A song inspired by events in Northern Ireland, then at the height of 'The Troubles', there is a dark, bleak mood about the piece. "I don't want to play the part, just a statistic on a Government chart," sings Sting about the need to escape from an urban hell as he imagines the pain of growing up amidst such violence. The single release reached Number Two in the UK but significantly the song wasn't put out in the States. There was considerable controversy when a video intended to accompany the single was banned from BBC TV's *Top Of The Pops* – a sign of the political and military tensions of the times. Unusually funky guitar from Andy shouts in anger above explosive cymbal crashes as Sting sings in low key his message of defiance and hope.

HUNGRY FOR YOU
(J'aurais toujours faim de toi)

Sting breaks into French during this strikingly funky work out built over a sonorous bass and guitar riff with Stewart stomping out a variety of back beats. The whole doomy effect is terrifyingly hypnotic and could in theory remain on constant play until the planets of the solar system cease revolving and orbit into the sun. Fortunately for our sanity the track is faded out on the orders of Commander Padgham.

DEMOLITION MAN

If the previous track was funky, this took The Police to new heights of grooviness. Sting sets up a bass guitar groove of monumental proportions, utilising a 'call and response' device that impinges on the consciousness like a Big Band swing riff. Andy adds layers of Clapton-esque blues guitar that recall a misspent youth in the Soho club scene of the Sixties. Stewart has fun showing how it's possible to lay down a snare drum off-beat while blazing away at his cymbals and tom-toms. As the vocals fade away it turns into a saxophone and guitar jam in the grand jazz tradition. And they have the cheek to start

it all over again, even after the sliders are drawn to complete a wrap. Sting wrote this while staying at actor Peter O'Toole's cottage one summer. Grace Jones recorded a version in 1981.

TOO MUCH INFORMATION

"Too much information going through my brain - driving me insane," says Sting bemoaning the overkill in news and info that was already swamping the world, even before the advent of Personal PCs, Teletext, Cable TV, Multi Media and The Internet. There is a hint of Caribbean rhythm and a touch of humour to soften the increasingly neurotic frenzy detected in the band's output at this time, doubtless induced by the pleasant location in Montserrat.

REHUMANIZE YOURSELF

In the battle against the machines, fascists and other blots on the landscape, Sting interprets Stewart Copeland's song that advises we find a source of common humanity. It's sung against a background of determined jollity heightened by Sting's honking saxophone. The lads sound like they are having fun on what is essentially a fast moving dance tune, ideal for weddings and limbo sessions.

ONE WORLD
(Not Three)

Clipped West Indian rhythms return with Ska type sax riffs, and a clever interplay between the bass drum and bass guitar that provides extraordinary lift. "One world is enough for all of us," is the message as the band jam out, Stewart offers knife edged drum fills. Exciting stuff.

OMEGAMAN

An Andy Summers' composition that has a quite different structure from more familiar Police material. It's distinguished by unusual chords, a brisk tempo and a rapid fade-out. Omega is the last letter in the Greek alphabet, so this doubtless refers to the last man to survive the human race.

SECRET JOURNEY

A spooky atmosphere prevails, redolent of rising mists and a moonlit landscape. This is very much a Sting song, full of his clever use of simple hooks contrasted by more complex passages. Not quite up to the standard of 'Message In A Bottle' however, and part of the 'dead zone' that lurks on even the best Police albums, rarely explored by stylus or scanned by laser.

DARKNESS

A better than average composition by Stewart Copeland that begins with warm, satisfying chords, a pleasant bass line, and busy hi-hats, before our singing star grooves into a laid back vocal performance that sounds not unlike the Lancastrian tones employed by Jon Anderson of Yes. It's strange, however, that the essential magic and direction of the band fades away and gets lost, whenever they play non-Sting material. Not a new discovery, but still doubtless a source of puzzlement and anguish to those who would have preferred The Police to be more democratic. However as Stewart and Andy would be the first to agree, Sting was undoubtedly their best composer. His material dominated The Police but as Andy Summers said: "There were hardly any broken hearts."

THE POLICE   SYNCHRONICITY

SYNCHRONICITY

(ORIGINAL UK RELEASE A&M, JUNE 1983; CD A&M CDA 63735 JUNE 1983)

When 'Synchronicity' burst upon the world, The Police seemed an unassailable force in popular music, and the band had everything to live for. However, few outside the organisation knew of the deep rooted antipathy that had developed between the highly individual, and talented, members. The rivalry for control of the band between Sting and Stewart seemed uncontainable and, both being powerful figures, neither would back down. Whether it was the speed of a performance, the use of a keyboard or a synthesiser, or the choice of a song, there always seemed plenty to argue and fight about.

As with the previous album, the band were undergoing pressures in their personal life, including the break up of marriages, and Sting of course was itching to start a solo recording career to match his work in films. Perhaps there was also the feeling they had done and said everything they could within The Police format. It had given them a framework, huge success and along the way they had created a mass of great music. But the spark of inspiration did not always ignite and Sting proclaimed: "As soon as it becomes a drag, then that's it – I walk out." And that's virtually what happened, after the release of 'Synchronicity'. They did start work on a follow up album due for release in 1984, but it never happened.

Work began on this album early in 1982, when Sting rented The Golden Eye estate in Jamaica, previously owned by Ian Fleming. The rock composer sat at the desk where Fleming wrote his James Bond stories and began composing the songs destined for 'Synchronicity'. At the end of the year the band convened at Montserrat, armed with some 20 songs on which they jammed together. The plan was to see which would work best and devise suitable arrangements. The most promising were by Sting as always, but they did include one by Stewart and another from Andy.

During a six-week period they worked hard on the material and it wasn't always easy. Andy Summers reported later that the title track was so hard to record, he and Stewart abandoned it to get a night's rest. The following morning they found Sting had laboured all night on the track, staying in the studio through the early hours, until it was ready. The song was of particular personal importance,

as it concerned his thoughts on the theories of philosopher Carl Jung. Sting had recently undertaken Jungian psychotherapy to cope with the traumas of a divorce.

Undoubtedly the finest song on the album was 'Every Breath You Take', which shone above the rest. The band helped Sting attain the right balance in their treatment of the song, combining spartan simplicity with underlying power. Andy Summer's guitar theme proved inspirational in the final treatment.

Both single and album topped the charts around the world. In the States 'Every Breath You Take' was Number One for eight weeks and the album stayed up there for an incredible 17 weeks, despite competition from Michael Jackson's mega-selling 'Thriller'. 'Every Breath' won a Grammy Award as Song Of The Year in 1984. Sting was proven right when he said: "I knew it would be a Number One hit!"

SYNCHRONICITY I

Speed, intensity and layers of hard riffing, make this a positive, powerful opener. Relentless, telegrammatic verses spit out lyrics about events occurring at the same time in different places. Such ideas were inspired by Sting's reading of the works of Carl Jung, the Swiss psychiatrist (1875-1961) who worked at a Zurich mental institute. It was Jung who coined the phrase 'complex' in his work *Studies In Word Association*. He remained a friend of Sigmund Freud until the pair broke up in 1913 over Freud's exclusively sexual definition of libido. From then on old

Carl developed his own theories of psychic energy, drawing on the dreams and drawings of his patients and embracing modern physics with his ideas about synchronicity. Sting sings of "a shared romance" and other facets of the mysteries of space, time and carnal lust.

WALKING IN YOUR FOOTSTEPS

A song about our native forebears, who 15 million years ago set forth on a journey that led to the creation of modern man. Flutes, sub-human howls and conga drums create a suitably primeval atmosphere. According to Sting our forebears were actually dinosaurs, but according to most history books Mankind did not actually share the planet with the dinosaurs, who died out long before the creators of fire, the wheel and computer games came on the scene. Nevertheless it remains a most unusual piece of work that breaks free of The Police mould.

O MY GOD

A return to older Police ideas, and you can hear overtones of 'The Bed's Too Big Without

You', and 'Demolition Man'. Sting sounds a bit throaty and strained, while the riffs, although played with firm insistence, have a strong sense of *déjà vu*. We certainly have been here before, but apart from the grim saxophone interlude, it's still a nice place to visit.

MOTHER

Summers at work and, sad to say, pretty ghastly stuff, with Andy shouting and screaming "The telephone is ringing. Is that my mother on the 'phone?" Psycho meets Talking Heads. Okay for a Robert Fripp album perhaps, but in the words of Nigel Tufnell of Spinal Tap – best forgotten.

MISS GRADENKO

Having almost destroyed the album with the last track, Andy is confined to a few tortured and random guitar notes which suggest he was undergoing some sort of inner crisis. Damage here is limited to a sub-standard Stewart Copeland song delivered with routine efficiency. "Is anybody alive in here? Nobody but us!" is the nub of the main theme. Grim.

SYNCHRONICITY II

After a strangely surreal intro, a Paul McCartney-ish mood prevails on a Sting song that revives the spirits and restores faith in the band. Here Stewart gets down to his job of bashing hell out of the drums, while Andy plays the guitar with all his old magical zeal and inspiration. Given the tools, they can finish the job. It's back to Carl Jung and his Rhythm Boys.

EVERY BREATH YOU TAKE

Every Police album had at least one or two super hit classics, and it was intriguing that 'Synchronicity', which proved to be their last and most uneven, spawned one of the finest songs of all. 'Every Breath You Take' is undoubtedly a masterpiece, perfectly constructed, flowing over a series of irresistible chords and blessed with a melody that brings out the best in Sting's voice. A moving, touching, lyrical idea, it never fails to tug at the heart strings and the song has become a great standard. Although superficially a tender romantic ballad, it also has depths of bitterness, as Sting muses on the love that turns to jealousy.

KING OF PAIN

Nothing can beat a simple song with minimal accompaniment for its effect on human emotions. Sting sounds like he's busy rehearsing for his forthcoming solo career with this piece. It begins with the voice complemented by a pedal piano motif. "There's a little black spot on the sun today," he says mysteriously, as a marimba clicks gently. "It's the same old thing as yesterday" he explains, as the band expounds the theme more briskly. Methinks he alludes to the blemishes in the hearts of man that tarnish the purity of love and emotion, and cause pain only to those who would seek undivided attention. That's my theory. Alternative views on postcards please.

WRAPPED AROUND YOUR FINGER

Although the band intended to reduce the 'Reggatta de Blanc' input on 'Synchronicity' this retains that Caribbean lilt, so redolent of rum, Coca-Cola and tax avoidance schemes. But this belittles an otherwise tender and imaginative song in which Sting is cast as the young apprentice seeking knowledge he would not otherwise find in college. This comes from a married woman, judging by the ring around her finger. "I will listen hard to your tuition," sings Sting over a sultry, sensuous rhythm. There's undoubtedly devil's work afoot.

TEA IN THE SAHARA

And so we say goodnight to The Police, at least in terms of purpose-made studio cuts. A plethora of B-sides and 'live' recordings were strewn in their wake, but this was the final curtain. A doomy farewell too, as Sting slips and slides into the mood created by a pulsating desert rhythm that suggests a camel making an uneven journey in the shadow of the pyramids. The title was inspired by a Paul Bowles novel *The Sheltering Sky*.

Andy Summers adds to the mood using an Echoplex effect on his guitar to summon images of shimmering heat. Sting later professed this was one of his favourite songs, although he felt it was played "too fast" on the album. Racing tempos was always a bone of contention between the warring factions of Sting and Stewart.

THE POLICE

GREATEST HITS

THE POLICE
GREATEST HITS

(A&M CD 5400302, RELEASED SEPTEMBER 1992)

The now standard Police 'Greatest Hits' album includes the following tracks: Roxanne, Can't Stand Losing You, So Lonely, Message In A Bottle, Walking On The Moon, The Bed's Too Big Without You, Don't Stand So Close To Me, De Do Do Do, De Da Da Da, Every Little Thing She Does Is Magic, Invisible Sun, Spirits In The Material World, Synchronicity II, Every Breath You Take, King Of Pain, Wrapped Around Your Finger, Tea In The Sahara.

In October 1986, this had been preceded by a similar selection entitled 'Every Breath You Take (The Singles)' (A&M CD EVECD1). Tracks were: Roxanne, Can't Stand Losing You, So Lonely, Message In A Bottle, Walking On The Moon, Don't Stand So Close To Me, De Do Do Do, De Da Da Da, Every Little Thing She Does Is Magic, Invisible Sun, Spirits In The Material World, Every Breath You Take, King Of Pain, Wrapped Around Your Finger, So Lonely.

MESSAGE IN A BOX
THE COMPLETE RECORDINGS
THE POLICE

MESSAGE IN A BOX

THE COMPLETE RECORDINGS
OF THE POLICE

(ORIGINAL UK RELEASE A&M 540 150-2 1993)

A limited edition digitally remastered 4 CD box set with every track The Police released, including their début single 'Fall Out' and a revised version of 'Don't Stand So Close To Me'. It also includes all the B-sides which didn't appear on albums and various live versions from New Wave compilations. A comprehensive illustrated book completes an excellent souvenir package, though it would have been nice to hear some more outtakes, unreleased songs and live material.

FULL TRACK LISTING AS FOLLOWS:

CD 1: 1. Fall Out 2. Nothing Achieving 3. Dead End Job 4. Next To You 5. So Lonely 6. Roxanne 7. Hole In My Life 8. Peanuts 9. Can't Stand Losing You 10. Truth Hits Everybody 11. Born In The 50's 12. Be My Girl-Sally 13. Masoko Tanga 14. Landlord (Live) 15. Next To You (Live) 16. Landlord 17. Message In A Bottle 18. Reggatta De Blanc 19. It's Alright For You 20. Bring On The Night 21. Deathwish

CD 2: 1. Walking On The Moon 2. On Any Other Day 3. The Bed's Too Big Without You 4. Contact 5. Does Everyone Stare 6. No Time This Time 7. Visions Of The Night 8. The Bed's Too Big Without You (Mono) 9. Truth Hits Everybody (Live) 10. Friends 11. Don't Stand So Close To Me 12. Driven To Tears 13. When The World Is Running Down, You Make The Best Of What's Still Around 14. Canary In A Coalmine 15. Voices Inside My Head 16. Bombs Away 17. De Do Do Do, De Da Da Da 18. Behind My Camel 19. Man In A Suitcase 20. Shadows In The Rain 21. The Other Way Of Stopping

CD 3: 1. A Sermon 2. Driven To Tears (Live) 3.Shambelle 4. Spirits In The Material World 5. Every Little Thing She Does Is Magic 6. Invisible Sun 7. Hungry For You (j'aurais toujours faim de toi) 8. Demolition Man 9. Too Much Information 10. Rehumanize Yourself 11. One World (Not Three) 12. Omegaman 13. Secret Journey 14. Darkness 15. Flexible Strategies 16. Low Life 17. How Stupid Mr.Bates 18. A Kind Of Loving

CD 4: 1. Synchronicity I 2. Walking In Your Footsteps 3. O My God 4. Mother 5. Miss Gradenko 6. Synchronicity II 7. Every Breath You Take 8. King Of Pain 9. Wrapped Around Your Finger 10. Tea In The Sahara 11. Murder By Numbers 12. Man In A Suitcase (Live) 13. Someone To Talk To 14. Message In A Bottle (Live) 15. I Burn For You 16. Once Upon A Daydream 17. Tea In The Sahara (Live) 18. Don't Stand So Close To Me '86

TRACKS NOT INCLUDED ON POLICE ALBUMS:

FALL OUT

The band's Do It Yourself style début single, released in 1977 at the height of the punk rock boom, and full of driving New Wave energy. It was the first song rehearsed by The Police and their first ever recording. Stewart Copeland actually plays the bulk of the guitar tracks, while Henri Padovani plays the main solo. As Stewart said: "When Andy joined the group, my guitar went back into the closet."

Sting later said about 'Fall Out': "It was entirely a tribute to Stewart's energy and focus." Difficult to remember now but The Police were totally obscure and unknown when they stormed their way into the clubs, with songs like 'Fall Out'. They certainly alarmed the other punks with their aggressive energy and skills.

NOTHING ACHIEVING

An angry bass riff launches Sting into a throaty battle cry. Even at his most punky he sings with a complexity and sophistication most vomit-stained gobsters of the period could barely conceive, let alone convey. Stewart's brother Ian wrote the lyrics with some additions from Sting and Stewart.

DEAD END JOB

"I don't want to be no teacher, don't want to be no slave!" snaps Sting on this high speed rave up – one of his favourite songs from the period. In those days of full employment people could complain about 'dead end job'. A couple of years into the Thatcher Eighties and most would have been grateful for any kind of job. Andy Summers reads out vacancy ads from a local paper in a Lancashire accent during the crazed climax. Apparently it was the only time Andy receive a compliment from Sting for his vocals.

Stewart devised the main riff, which he'd kept on hold since High School days. John Cale produced an earlier version of the song, but this one features Andy Summers on guitar.

LANDLORD

A live version of a super fast rave up that buzzes with electrifying zest, verve and power! In many ways it was a shame The Police didn't retain this kind of simplicity. They might have been happier little superstars if they hadn't got lost among the 'Jungian blue camels of the desert'. Stewart wrote the riff while Sting's lyrics were a direct reaction to being thrown out of a house he and his wife Frances had been renting in London. "Stay out of your seats!" Stewart warns the fans as he cues the band into action. Well The Police are famous for giving orders. Andy's frenetic solo would have astounded Zoot Money's Big Roll Band.

NEXT TO YOU
(Live)

A rough-edged, angry, high speed version of the pogo-rocker first heard on 'Outlandos d'Amour.' It's a tad garbled but you can hear the desperation to impress America coming through the barrage of drum and guitar thunder. "Goodnight New York City" yells Sting, as he introduces the band. Exhausted and breathless he blurts out a brief "Thank you Bottom Line," before launching into a relentless reprise of the chorus, complete with an explosive drum finale. You can almost feel the band's hot breath down your neck during this authentically sweaty on-the-spot recording. It's said the original lyrics by Andy and Stewart were rather more aggressive, but Sting introduced a love motif into proceedings. Said Stewart: "We didn't mind the love lyrics, as long as he shouted them aggressively!"

LANDLORD

In the studio version the guitars squeal like Morse Code and the tempo accelerates at a rate no producer would permit in this age of drum machine domination.

Sting, from his position as an impoverished youth, launches into an attack on the middle class and middle aged, those philistine parasites then blighting his life. The guitar coda is pure blues.

VISIONS OF THE NIGHT

Sting's first song written after arriving in London from Newcastle. It has a certain rough charm, and it is interesting to hear The Who influence, a touch of Townshend/Daltrey perhaps, in their 'Quadrophenia' period. The usual punk grind is interspersed with interesting off-the-wall ideas, enhanced by Andy's imaginative guitar work which never relied on the obvious, even on the most basic material.

THE BED'S TOO BIG WITHOUT YOU
(Mono)

"All I made was one mistake – now the bed's too big – without YOU" squeals Sting in best reggae mode, interpreting those very personal lyrics that seem to strike a chord in the coldest of hearts. The first version on 'Reggatta De

Blanc' swells into action, while this has more direct impact. The bass line is allowed to glide more ominously while Stewart improvises on hi-hats, and Andy sustains a deft, uplifting reggae rhythm.

TRUTH HITS EVERYBODY
(Live)

The Police were sustaining their angry, high speed groove, taking their cue from the spiky-haired, as they tore into this live version of the song from 'Outlandos d'Amour.'

Intriguing to hear Sting and Stewart clashing over the introduction, as "Nice to be back" is interrupted by a spirited "1,2,3,4!" Sting takes care with the lyrics despite the hubbub of a gig situation, and keen students of the drums will note Stewart's ankle breaking bass drum work. Guitarists will lust after Andy's howling crescendo.

FRIENDS

Andy Summers adopts a country bumpkin accent, predating *Silence Of The Lambs* by several years as he announces "I likes to

eat my friends – I make no bones about it."
A strange business, that Andy himself
describes as "A touch of Long John Silver on
acid." Andy claims he wrote it after having
read Robert Heinlein's sci-fi novel *Stranger In
A Strange Land*.

A SERMON

Strange how the influence of The Who can be
heard so often in the early work, most notably
in the shouting, slightly erratic vocals. It's a bit
like Daltrey and Townshend having an argu-
ment on stage. Surprisingly drummer
Copeland plays the main guitar riff, his style
perfectly suited to the Ramones-ish groove.
The lyrics bellow about newly famous rock
stars abusing all and sundry, having paid their
dues and seeking an arrogant form of revenge.

DRIVEN TO TEARS
(Live)

Interesting variations on the studio version can
be heard on this spooky, floating 'live' rendition
of a song Sting wrote whilst on the road, as
opposed to being created in some distant farm

house. Andy Summers takes an excellent guitar solo, short but packed with passion. "We
only ever let him have 8-bars," said Sting later.
Apart from the solo, Sting says what he most
remembers about the gig was threatening to
kill someone in the front row who threw a
stone at him.

SHAMBELLE

An excellent Andy Summers instrumental
composition, which doubtless went some way
to compensate for his solo restrictions on
stage. Sting sets up a repetitive bass line,
while Andy devotes most of his playing to
chordal expositions of the eerie theme. The
B-sides of those singles where tracks like
'Shambelle' popped up, gave Andy a chance
to experiment with new ideas, once he had
gotten Stewart and Sting's co-operation.

FLEXIBLE STRATEGIES

Echoing off-beats from Stewart and funky guitar riffs herald a solid Police jam session that
took place in Canada. The band had been
ordered to create a B-side in a hurry and this

was the result. Stewart opined that it was "a disgrace", but if you like hearing a band of great musicians getting their rocks off without trying to get a hit, this is a joy, especially when they break into double time.

LOW LIFE

"Fatal fascination for the seedy part of town," sings Sting. "Don't be seen alone without your friends at night. Take a gun or a knife to meet the low life." Excellent lyrics, clearly enunciated in best bluesy style without recourse to vocal trickery. Olaf Kubler, a jazzman they'd met while working with Eberhard Schoener in Germany, provides a jazzy saxophone solo. It's interesting to note that neither Andy nor Stewart particularly liked this tune at the time, although it was said to be one of Sting's favourites. Stewart felt the use of a sax detracted from their main aim of establishing an identifiable Police sound. In a sense he was right for this was an unconscious rehearsal for the Blue Turtles to come. (Andy? Stewart? Sounds like a recipe for Scottish country dancing.)

HOW STUPID MR.BATES

The Police provided music for the soundtrack of the TV film *Brimstone & Treacle* in which Sting played a leading role as the character Martin. This is suitably nondescript background atmospheric stuff, which all makes sense seen against a background of establishing shots, or more preferably in this case, against fast forwarded closing credits.

A KIND OF LOVING

Another segment from *Brimstone & Treacle*. Lots of hideous female screaming suggests torture and torment, with accompanying cries of 'Shut up!' all doubtless deemed suitable for Mr.Dennis Potter's celebrated television drama. Both these tracks should have been bulk erased by a public spirited engineer.

MURDER BY NUMBERS

Sting's classic jazz roots to the fore on this excellent smoky cabaret club number, enhanced by Andy Summers' magnificent choice of chords. Desultory applause completes the languid atmosphere.

MAN IN A SUITCASE
(Live)

A quite different feel prevails on this live performance of a song first heard on 'Zenyatta Mondatta.'

SOMEONE TO TALK TO

Now here's a rarity, an Andy Summers vocal that works quite well, mainly because he sings properly without adopting a silly accent. His style is warm and pleasant and he establishes a kind of innocence with these unpretentious lyrics. He emotes regret over yet another failed relationship. Andy was disappointed that Sting wouldn't sing this particular song, but then the lyrics are fearfully personal.

MESSAGE IN A BOTTLE
(Live)

Always one of the band's own personal favourites, they play 'Message' with a mixture of care, restraint and fire, ignited in the heat of the moment. Gone is the ragged sound of the early punk Police, and the band fade themselves out to enable Sting to gently repeat the

hook line, before they burst back into action for the famed "Ye-oh!" routine. The band played this tune at Sting's wedding some ten years after they broke up. What was the message – two pints please?

I BURN FOR YOU

A romantic, sensitive song that Sting wrote in a classroom back in his Newcastle days. He managed to write the words while setting his pupils a long piece of work. Pizzicato strings pluck a sensuous introduction as Sting launches into a superb performance that sensibly should have been included on 'Zenyatta Mondatta' but Sting withdrew the piece after objections from Stewart and Andy.

First played by Sting with Last Exit during their residency at the Gosforth Hotel in Newcastle, it was later performed 'live' with The Police, once Stewart felt they could afford to soften up a bit. During the final chorus the band launch unexpectedly into a kind of Men O'The Mountains chant, the sort of thing Vikings might have sung while hauling logs to construct their next longboat.

ONCE UPON A DAYDREAM

Another fine 'lost' song, with beautiful chords supplied by Andy Summers and lyrics courtesy of Gordon Sumner. It was written by a swimming pool in Montserrat during the band's 'Ghost In The Machine' period. It's the sort of song you'd imagine Doris Day singing in a Walt Disney movie – one of Walt's darker productions.

TEA IN THE SAHARA
(Live)

An extended version of the last track on the 1983 'Synchronicity' album, this piece grows on the listener with repeated plays and the 'live' version particularly helps the rest of us understand why it became one of Sting's favourites. There's lots of space, and plenty of Echoplex-aided guitar work.

Only the faint whistles of the distant crowd of hot and impatient rockers in the audience, give away that this is performed on stage and not in a studio. The lyrics are about broken promises and were inspired by the book *The Sheltering Sky*, by Paul Bowles, that Andy once lent Sting. Never lend books – you never get them back.

DON'T STAND SO CLOSE TO ME '86

A somewhat shocking glimpse into an unfathomable future, the sound of The Police in the mid-Eighties. The digitised, machine-tooled accuracy is cold, and harsh compared to the ebbing and flowing life of 'Tea In The Sahara'. It's the heartless sound of the robot generation, in which one android wouldn't know if another android was standing too close to him, unless there was a slight *frisson* of electronic interference. Andy Summers plays a very human guitar solo, but the rest sounds like a ghost in the machine. Despite, or perhaps because of the apparent hostility that existed between the band members during this abortive attempt to record a new album, the vocals have a greater poignancy than was evident on the original.

THE POLICE LIVE!

(ORIGINAL UK RELEASE A&M 540 222-2 MAY 1995)

For many years fans lusted after a 'live' album from The Police that would recapture the excitement and zest of the band in concert. There had been a few 'live' cuts on The Police Boxed Set, but in 1995, a decade after the band split up, came the full aural evidence. This double CD set commemorates two full tilt American concerts that span the opening and closing days of the band's career. The drive and drama of these performances show the band were just as good as fond memory suggests. Disc One of the set is devoted to a show at the Orpheum, Boston, originally broadcast by WBCN in November 1979, and includes 15 explosive versions of songs from their 'Reggatta de Blanc' period, complete with "noises off" and verbal asides from the troublesome trio.

Disc Two is devoted to a concert from their 'Synchronicity' period recorded at The Omni, Atlanta, Georgia, in November 1983, with a further 15 action packed tracks. The show gives a unique insight into a band hard at work, sweating to make it happen, each musician giving his utmost, with that competitive edge adding a spark of danger to proceedings. They were so good, it was a shame they had to end up fighting, but that is invariably the case with practically every rock band that has ever amounted to more than a pile of beans. One thinks of The Beatles, The Who and The Cream as prime examples of engines of self destruction. Only the Bert Wilcox Five of Neasden never had so much as a cross word in 35 years, and apart from Mrs.Wilcox, who buys their albums?

DISC ONE:

NEXT TO YOU

Conflict emerges almost instantaneously, as both Stewart and Sting shout a greeting to the cheering hordes. This conflicting exchange

THE POLICE LIVE! : POLICE

establishes just who is in charge of this band – ME! A few bars into the performance the engineer awakes and turns up the faltering volume level. However it's fun to hear these glitches, rather like the lightning that used to interrupt Swing broadcasts from the Thirties and is now captured permanently on album.

SO LONELY

"I feel so lonely!" yells Sting communicating with his audience. "I'm not surprised," snaps Stewart with unnecessary rudeness from behind his drums. "Chaw chaw," retorts Sting, which shows just what he thinks of this impertinence. Andy Summers rises above all this backstage stuff and plays with an attacking violence and range of ideas never given free rein on the confines of the original albums. As Sting begins to extemporise over the theme, you can hear the throaty quality of his voice that sounds as if it is under attack from swamp fever, thick fog, too many cigarettes and a serious sore throat. It's a frailty that gives his voice such charm and appeal. When he doesn't have to shout above the band, he displays an extraordinary degree of control over his vocal emo-

tions, using his voice like a saxophone to hit the highest notes.

A brilliant performance, and you can actually hear Stewart offering an encouraging cry of "Nice going."

TRUTH HITS EVERYBODY
(Live)

First heard on the 'Message In A Box' set, the introduction gives away internal battles as certain members of the band both try to make announcements. Adopting the role of the Fat Promoter, you feel like yelling from the VIP seats, "Hey you guys, sort it out. Who's running this band anyway?" Such musings aside, this is full of crisp cut excitement.

WALKING ON THE MOON

'This is from my new record," says Sting rather shamelessly. Not 'our' new record, note. Ah well, 'Walking On The Moon' was his idea, but doubtless such pronouncements led Stewart to flick peanuts off the back of his singer's head. Once again Andy's guitar shines with a bounce and clarity not detected on the album version, and it is instructive to note that Sting plays the tricky bass line, while coping with vocal couplets, no easy task we can be sure. Copeland's stick work is a joy behind Sting's brief 'Yo, yo, yo' excursion. The crowd don't quite know how to react to this 'new' song. A few months later and they would all be yelling their heads off.

HOLE IN MY LIFE

A touch of the Paul McCartneys about the bass line on this rather under-rated item in The Police repertoire, which builds with hypnotic power, before hitting a series of land mine explosions – or 'breaks' as they have it in jazz circles. The audience are driven wild by this cunning interplay.

FALL OUT

Their first single, and still in the set to celebrate their punk roots and provide a bit of uplift in the middle of a show. It's fast, fun and gives Andy a chance to rock out with ferocious zeal. Most guitar bands tend to fall apart or over play at such tempos, but The Police keep it tightly under control.

BRING ON THE NIGHT

Andy Summers once again surpasses himself with some superb chords, gently sustained in an undulating riff that alternates with a lilting reggae pattern, before entering another dimension of space and time. Sting restricts himself to a few lines, giving his voice a rest and allowing Andy room for expression.

MESSAGE IN A BOTTLE

Once again the Bostonians don't seem quite prepared for this classic, having just arrived on the Greyhound bus and still ordering their bags of popcorn. But the magical qualities of the song, played a tad too fast for comfort, quickly grips the audience who are privy to a brilliant young band in the throes of creating musical history. "Sending out an S.O.S." chorus the band, with Sting enunciating the phrase rather more carefully than on the studio version.

THE BED'S TOO BIG WITHOUT YOU

Another treat for concert-goers, hearing perhaps for the first time this neatly arranged

reggae tinged song of loneliness. Sting makes love to his pillow and bemoans the heartache of separation.

The bass and guitar embark on a comforting duet in which empty space is filled with cascading sheets of sound. Sting's prowess as a bassman is clearly defined, while Stewart shows how to express musical ideas on a drum kit without ever playing the obvious. The interplay between all three here is quite inspired, and shows that whatever the aggravations on the road, when it came to making music, only friendship prevailed. The hypnotic ending, which Sting holds together in the teeth of inane yells from the usual bozos who attend rock concerts, has all the pristine purity of a piece of fine china.

PEANUTS

Bozo placation afoot here, as the band snap into some rapid fire unison rock that keeps the restless elements happy, and allows some physical activity (to whit, pogo-ing) before there is a need to settle down and hopefully listen once more.

ROXANNE

Wonderful of course, but rather over familiar. What makes this particularly interesting is the long and daring passages where drums, bass and guitar are virtually silent before Sting brings the piece back to life. In an age when most punk and even long-in-the-tooth hard rockers dared not stop making a din for a moment in case of "losing" their audience, The Police just showed their confidence and intelligence with their use of dynamics. It was a wise old muso who uttered those immortal words: "It's not what you play, but what you don't play that counts."

CAN'T STAND LOSING YOU

Indeed this is a most enjoyable concert, and perhaps one of the finest, most satisfying rock shows on record since The Who's 'Live At Leeds', lately re-released in extended form. As Sting yells out his introduction, the tight little, right little trio evince an eagerness that instantly communicates itself to the crowd.

The tension and excitement rises and the audience responds with an enthusiasm that goes beyond mere conditioned reflex.

LANDLORD

Ramming speed now as the band go punk and still manage to make it sound exciting and interesting, something few authentic punk bands could ever achieve. Summer's chords shimmer like heat rising.

BORN IN THE 50's

"1,2,3,4,5,6" shouts Sting quaintly, bringing the chaps into one of their least effective songs. Who needed the tedious Fifties when The Police were patently a band for the much more exciting Eighties? The lyrics are relentlessly naff and the theme weak and unworthy of the band. However, it makes a fairly undemanding piece to usher in an encore after an exhausting set.

BE MY GIRL/SALLY

Andy's music hall style monologue about an inflatable doll is delivered in a strained Lancashire accent, much to the baffled amusement of the crowd. Mercifully the band came back for a reprise of 'Next To You.'

SYNCHRONICITY II

The lyrics have as much impact as the studio version, despite the racing tempo and finely tuned thunder of The Police engines revving at full throttle. The structure of the piece survives this flip performance intact, although it could have been delivered with greater attention to mood.

DISC TWO:

SYNCHRONICITY I

A few years later and they're still shouting "1,2,3!" but there is a detectable change in the sound of the band at this 1983 show. Smoother perhaps, slicker and less erratic. This fast paced conception from their last studio album has a ghostly and mysterious quality underpinned by a relentless beat. Copeland's bass drum is heavier and steadier, the vocal harmonies are better synchronised and the ensemble playing has greater power. Another difference between Boston and Atlanta lies in the roar of the crowd – more people, more adulation.

WALKING IN YOUR FOOTSTEPS

Now the group get into their stride, although there is a rather curious "snore" from Sting a few lines into the lyric, which suggests he was peeved about something.

It sounds like they're using a drum machine in the background as a click track, and some funky backing vocalists help Sting sustain a gospel groove. Rather than seek out imperfections or try to read significance into the slightest deviations on these unique performances, it is probably best to let it all wash over you, and like the audience, simply enjoy everything you hear and take it on face value.

MESSAGE IN A BOTTLE

Well worth repeating, as there are enough differences in Sting's delivery, and the band's treatment. Piercing screams penetrate the sound mix as the youth of Atlanta see their pin-ups given life and flesh. (An expert whistler in the crowd makes his lips ache as he greets the climax.)

O MY GOD

Echoes of 'Demolition Man' as Sting slugs out an irresistible bass riff, and locks into a funky groove as the backing singers Tessa Niles, Dolette McDonald and Michelle Cobbs give it some. Great stuff and a new slant on a possible future for the band, if only they'd had the common sense to keep it all going. "Fill it up!" orders the boss. What can he mean? Are we to suppose there are sexual connotations to all this rhythmic foreplay?

DE DO DO DO, DE DA DA DA

A kind of hugging warmth surrounds their big US hit. Incidentally, as we progress through

the concert we hear Sting clearly in charge of proceedings and there are no more gauche interruptions and shouts from the drummer. The drumming is more contained and Andy's guitar is less frantic. Maturity is the phrase that lurches all too readily to mind.

WRAPPED AROUND YOUR FINGER

It is still worth pointing out the three-piece remains perhaps the most effective line-up in rock, certainly from the evidence of this stunningly beautiful exercise in atmospherics. The words hang like steamy breath in cold air, and the guitar and drums offer all the kind of selfless support and tonal variety that one might expect from a large orchestra. It's during moments like this that one realises just what a huge hole the absence of The Police has left in contemporary music.

TEA IN THE SAHARA

This moody, surreal exploration was overlooked amidst the hubbub that surrounded The Police during its final days. Certainly the discerning have claimed it as one of their favourites, and those who missed its significance the first time around can enjoy its subtleties fully expressed on this magical version.

Stewart's cymbals dance with a sunshine brilliance as Andy's guitar sobs and heaves in muted distress. It sounds like Sting is blowing an Arabian pipe picked up on a shopping trip to the bazaar, in the final exquisite moments.

SPIRITS IN THE MATERIAL WORLD

Although there is surprisingly little *reggatta de blanc* evident during these historic concerts, considering the fuss made over it at the time, this is undoubtedly the closest they get to the spirit of Bob Marley. The main theme is delivered with a punishing rock beat that drives to a brisk coda greeted with delighted applause.

KING OF PAIN

"There's a little black spot on the sun today," sings our Geordie lad, holding the audience in the palm of his hand.

He almost snarls "the King of Pain" as he pours heart and soul into another demanding, difficult song. Not an easy task being a lead singer, when you've got meaningful, complex lyrics to deliver night after night, with always the risk of a half consumed hamburger flying through the air at the crucial moment, followed by the review in the local paper next day. "Pop star Sting bored this writer stiff with a real dull show at the Omni last night. Fortunately The Ramones are in town next week… " Cyrus T.Weismuller, rock and baseball correspondent, *Atlanta Chronicle*.

DON'T STAND SO CLOSE TO ME

A teasing preview of the theme pierces the air, then young Master Sting addresses the riotous hordes, keeping his class under control with one of the sexiest songs of temptation ever devised. "Strong words in the staff room, the accusations fly" warbles Sting invoking the plight of the teacher pushed by circumstances up against a tempting lass clad only in a short skirt and white blouse with stocking tops peeping out from beneath her… control Smithers, control.

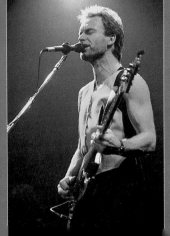

EVERY BREATH YOU TAKE

By George! This Sting fellow certainly came up with a string of excellent songs in his youth. Was he possessed, one wonders? Some have suggested witchcraft at work, or perhaps the use of illegal substance. There can be few other plausible explanations for the existence of this minor masterpiece. But why stint on praise when it's due? A major masterpiece.

ROXANNE

It is an unfortunate tendency among rock 'groups' to indulge in dubious subject matter. Take for example 'Roxanne.' Not only has Sting admitted having visited the Red Light district of Paris, but he wrote a song about a prostitute as a direct result of his observations. No wonder the BBC banned it from their wireless broadcasting stations. Unmitigated filth, but one has to allow it has a certain charm.

CAN'T STAND LOSING YOU

During the last performance a certain loss of that brittle spontaneity that illuminated their early work is noted and here the backing vocals actually get in the way rather than enhance the piece. It sounds mundane and less meaningful once the essential chemistry of the group is adulterated by outside elements. A fanciful supposition but there might be a germ of truth in it. Andy clangs his guitar with an unexpected touch of heavy metal, as Sting starts on the long uphill task of getting the audience to sing along.

SO LONELY

This is where we came in. Time to check the exits and try and get out before the car park jams up. But just a minute, Sting is going into his long rap and the smoke and the light show is going into overdrive, so you can't possibly leave until the last moments. Andy is playing one of his elliptical solos, and Stewart is kicking ass. This is The Police as we love them, but now it's all over and we start the long drive home knowing we'll never see another band like them again. More's the pity. We may have uttered a few critical words and harsh judgement along the way during our journey through the heartland of this unique band, but music without flaws or bones of contention is a lifeless, worthless thing. The Police were ever alive and worth every minute, as this particular souvenir only confirms.

THE DREAM OF THE BLUE TURTLES

(ORIGINAL UK RELEASE A&M, JUNE 1985; CD A&M 393 750-2 JUNE 1985)

In 1985 The Police had still not officially disbanded, but were put on ice while their lead singer busied himself with an increasingly hectic personal schedule. He maintained his work as a much in-demand movie actor, appearing notably in the singularly unpleasant film of Frank Herbert's sci-fi novel *Dune*.

At the same time he set about fulfilling his dreams, perhaps nurtured since his days as a struggling musician in Newcastle, of getting himself a real 'live' New York jazz band. Except, of course, it was not intended to be an all-out improvising jazz combo in the traditional sense. Sting wanted the best players to help interpret his new songs with the feeling and passion only the best jazz musicians can offer. He'd give them space to express themselves, but at the same time impose the formal discipline of song structures and arrangements. It was Sting's great achievement, not easily attained, of balancing the input of the self-contained musician with his own ideas about lyrics, melodies and concepts.

He already had a taste of solo success with a cover of the old standard 'Spread A Little Happiness' from the soundtrack of the movie *Brimstone &Treacle*. It had been a hit in September 1982 and augured well for the future. Then in January 1985 he began holding auditions for a new backing group in New York.

The following month he formed The Blue Turtles Band with Kenny Kirkland (keyboards), Branford Marsalis (saxophones), Omar Hakim (drums) and Darryl Jones (bass). These fine musicians all had an impressive pedigree. Branford and his trumpet star brother Wynton were giants on their respective instruments and spearheaded the new wave of highly trained musicians who graced the contemporary jazz scene. Branford had played with Art Blakey and Dizzy Gillespie. Omar Hakim had played with jazz-rock band Weather Report, and Darryl Jones had worked with Miles Davis (and would go on to effectively replace Bill Wyman in The Rolling Stones). Kenny Kirkland had played keyboard with Wynton Marsalis, Gillespie and Elvin Jones. This astonishingly eclectic and talented band made its début appearance at New York's Ritz.

Work then began on 'The Dream Of The Blue Turtles' at Eddie Grant's Blue Wave studio in Barbados. The album was released in June 1985 and swiftly topped charts on both sides of the Atlantic.

Although not perhaps as readily accessible as the punk-reggae brashness of The Police, the more sophisticated style crept up and ingratiated itself with an impressed public. Of course Sting's superstar status ensured the album's rapid conquest of the charts. It remains a source of pleasure to hear, a decade on.

An album that repays close attention to detail, it has a wealth of subtleties and passing delights. Although there are few instant brassy pop hits, there are mature compositions, some

genuinely moving in their patent sincerity and impressive in their sharpness of intellect. 'Russians' and 'Children's Crusade' are both a long way from 'De Do Do Do.' And yet the first two songs are curiously disappointing, perhaps cunningly placed at the beginning of the album as a sort of tease, to allow the full strength of Sting's ultimate commitment and vision to penetrate and play upon the senses with greater impact.

IF YOU LOVE SOMEBODY SET THEM FREE

In throaty, soulful style, Sting embarks on his great voyage into relatively uncharted solo waters, rather under using his all-star band on this routine pop soul work-out. On first impression, they sound like a superior weddings and bar mitzvah band, competent but unexceptional. The lyrics exude a cold streak of selfishness. 'If You Love Somebody' was released as a single and reached Number 26 in the UK charts but was a much bigger hit in the States where it got to Number 3 in *Billboard* in June.

LOVE IS THE
SEVENTH WAVE

Without the probing, restless urgency of his
old Police colleagues behind him, and without
the uncomfortable sense of competition, the
music tends to float into a Caribbean sea of
complacency. Comfort and ease rather than
angst and fire. However, it's a pleasant enough
ditty, distinguished by touches of soprano sax,
and the lyrical message of love against the war
machine is stronger than first appears. Sting
brings this sugar coated pill to life at the end
with a lugubrious ad lib: "Every breath you
take, every cake you bake…"

RUSSIANS

After the weakness of the preceding tracks, 'Russians' leaps out all the more strongly as a song worthy of Sting's talent and reputation. It's a powerful, simple, heartfelt plea for sanity and common sense in world affairs, at a time of heightened international tension. The song recalls the growing belligerence of the 'Evil Empire' years under the Reagan administration.

Sting recalls the chilling words of Kruschev's "We will bury you" speech at the height of the Cold War, and says "I hope the Russians love their children too." It's not *entirely* implausible to suggest that this innocent remark may not have fallen on *entirely* deaf ears.

CHILDREN'S CRUSADE

Sting sustains the writing standards achieved on 'Russians', elevating the pop song into something of value and importance in the process with his restrained, understated observation about the horrors of the First World War. He offers a surprising twist, comparing the poppies that were symbols of sacrifice in the war torn trenches of 1914, with the opium poppies that represent another betrayal – the destruction of drug torn youth in the present day.

SHADOWS IN THE RAIN

At last the band is given its head to blow, and sax man Branford Marsalis wails. "Wait - what key is this in?" demands the voice of a disgruntled musician as the drums kick in, and a sense of impatience and panic momentarily grips the band before it all drops into place. It's nice to hear that Sting actually stops singing long enough to allow the keyboard player and sax man to solo, an alien concept amongst most singers who think nothing is happening unless they are constantly warbling away. Large sections of the public would prefer to sit back and enjoy hearing collective music making.

WE WORK THE BLACK SEAM

During the mid-Eighties the great debate raged over the closure of pits and the destruction of the mining industry as coal was phased out in favour of nuclear power. Sting manages to turn an economic debate into a heartfelt and romantically disposed view of the human cost – on the miners of his native North East of England. He points out that coal dust is being replaced by Carbon 14, deadly, we are told, for 12,000 years. Boy they are gonna love us in the 25th Century. A steam shovel beats and provides an appropriately industrial backing.

CONSIDER ME GONE

A lightly swinging piece with a cool jazz groove leaves space for some expressive tenor sax. Sting contemplates the sense of emptiness left by a broken relationship and once again the lyrics are embellished by words carefully chosen for their expressive and suggestive powers, as befits an actor.

THE DREAM OF THE BLUE TURTLES

A brief instrumental interlude capped with studio laughter, left on the album as light relief from the more serious songs. It's a brief nod to the tradition of live music making, in a

recording era increasingly at the mercy of the producer and the machine.

MOON OVER BOURBON STREET

A remarkable piece, on which Sting sings *sotto voce* at first before embarking on a course of rising tension in the grand cabaret manner. A bowed bass note from the man himself concludes an exquisite vignette graced by fine saxophone playing. The bass player says the piece was inspired by *Interview With A Vampire* by Anne Rice.

FORTRESS AROUND YOUR HEART

Curiously enough, at the album's end we find the only piece that harks back to The Police, still then fresh in the memory and open for a possible reunion. There is something about the Copeland style back beat and the lyrical structure that recalls the heady days of 'Walking On The Moon' although the resemblance is only superficial. The allegorical lyrics are another story. A Top Twenty hit in the States.

STING: Bring on the Night

M. Le Sting et les Tortues Bleus'

BRING ON THE NIGHT

(ORIGINAL UK RELEASE A&M 396 705-2 JUNE 1986)

This 'live' double album was released to accompany a Grammy-winning documentary film *Bring On The Night* directed by Michael Apted and shot during a concert in Paris, in December 1985. It features Sting's new band in full cry, stretching out and soloing with a freedom not permissible within the relatively tight strictures of the 'Blue Turtles' album. Tracks on the CD were culled from various concerts in Paris, Arnhem and Rome during December.

Sting allows himself the pleasure of re-working some of his old Police favourites on stage, including 'Bring On The Night', 'When The World Is Running Down', 'Demolition Man' and 'Tea In The Sahara'. The rest of the material is from 'The Dream Of The Blue Turtles'. While the CD is full of great music and riveting performances, the actual packaging leaves much to be desired. A combination of studied 'throwaway' style design, including childish paintings and graphics, together with the minuscule type sizes make the information unreadable without heavy duty magnifying glasses. In fact most of Sting's CD covers have careless, sloppy designs, none of which reflect the care and thought that goes into the music.

Just when this album was being released The Police made a surprise reappearance for a reunion concert in Atlanta, on July 11, at the end of an Amnesty International all-star tour. The band played five songs and it was their last public appearance.

The following month they tried to record a sixth album together, but the London sessions came to nothing, and the band broke up after eight years of achievement, enormous success and constant pressure. Sting was free to sing, play and write, without the need to fight for his place in the sun.

BRING ON THE NIGHT/ WHEN THE WORLD IS RUNNING DOWN YOU MAKE THE BEST OF WHAT'S STILL AROUND

The poppy flavour of the original is quickly abandoned (mercifully) as the rhythm section begins to cook and Sting begins to scat sing and improvise. 'Bring On The Night' was first recorded by The Police in 1978 and the song itself was written three years earlier. The excitement snaps into play as the band segue into 'When The World Is Running Down' from 'Zenyatta Mondatta.'

Said Sting: "The two tunes share a chord sequence and a post-apocalyptic vision... such vanity as to imagine one's self as the sole survivor of a holocaust with all one's favourite things still intact!"

Suddenly a powerful authentic rap voice emerges in the midst of Kenny Kirkland's superb piano solo. It's Branford Marsalis showing how it should be done. This eleven minute epic is a joyous celebration of all that's best about contemporary music, and a reminder of what can be achieved when artists from different backgrounds can be brought together in common cause.

CONSIDER ME GONE

A wonderfully slow groove burns like a fuse as Omar Hakim floats gently on his ride cymbal and Sting sings in coolly elegant mode. It's notable that he abandons many of the over-the-top mannerisms that embellished his work with The Police and sings in a style suited to the maturity of his new playmates. Again - Mr.Sumner sounds not unlike the Jon Anderson of very early Yes, when Bill Bruford was making them swing. Cheers from the wildly enthusiastic and attentive French crowd greet the unbearably slick coda as Sting offers a grateful "Merci bien".

LOW LIFE

A bit like Hall & Oates with its blue eyed soul sound, rendered more interesting by Omar Hakim's drum fills and the constant flow of fine tenor sax work. The piece was originally written in the back of a tour bus on the way to a gig in 1977. Recalled the composer: "We'd just spent a week in a hotel on the Reeperbahn, Hamburg's red light district. Every lonely face tells a story, including mine I suppose."

STING : BRING ON THE NIGHT

WE WORK THE BLACK SEAM

The miners' lament from 'Blue Turtles' brought to life and taken at a slighter faster clip. Said Sting: "The melody for 'Black Seam' has lain among my notes for perhaps ten years. I could never finish it or find a suitable lyric until the miners' strike and a long talk with a friend who has a job trying to mend nuclear power stations with gaffa tape."

DRIVEN TO TEARS

This was written in 1979 in a US motel while Sting was watching the news on TV and saw pictures of children starving, with legs too weak to support them. Said Sting: "Tears of rage were one thing but Band Aid was better." Branford Marsalis takes off with an extended soprano solo.

THE DREAM OF THE BLUE TURTLES/DEMOLITION MAN

The wonderfully jazzy introduction has shades of Frank Zappa and overtones of *West Side Story*, with its staccato theme. The arrangement slots effortlessly into the menacing, hypnotic thunder of 'Demolition Man' from 'Ghost In The Machine'. Hakim picks up the tempo in time for Sting to sing with uncharacteristic gruffness.

ONE WORLD (NOT THREE)/LOVE IS THE SEVENTH WAVE

"It may seem a million miles away but it gets a little closer every day," chortles Sting and his merry men in a remarkable choral introduction before the band drops into a reggae beat enlivened by a lilting marimba rhythm. Complete with a creamy and richly melodic soprano solo, this performance underlines the extraordinary versatility of a band that must have given Sting enormous pride and pleasure.

Hours of rehearsal must have gone into the construction of the apparently effortless vocal riffing that blends the two songs.

MOON OVER BOURBON STREET

Sting wrote this cunningly arranged piece one night in the French Quarter of New Orleans in

1983. Branford Marsalis upstages Sting with his playful impressions of Sidney Bechet on his trusty soprano sax. Too good for rock-'n'roll fans. No wonder Sting was sometimes accused of arrogance during the Eighties when he seemed to conquer all. He's a clever bastard, you've got to admit. Nice looks, jolly tunes and not bad on the banjo either.

I BURN FOR YOU

Vibraphone notes introduce a song written by Sting in his classroom during a maths lesson way back in 1975. He recalls that he was then in a band that had a weekly residency in a Newcastle pub. He had to provide them with a flow of new songs and the only way he could find time to write was to set his pupils long maths tests.

"This kept them quiet and allowed me the relative solitude I needed to cobble together lines and music," recalls Sting. The song was used on the soundtrack of *Brimstone & Treacle* in which he played the Devil. Sting reports that the soundtrack won a Grammy Award… and the kids got their 'O' levels.

ANOTHER DAY

Described by Sting as 'a despondent song' with pointed, pertinent lyrics, nevertheless he gets his audience singing along in Phil Collins' style and the rhythm section cook some driving soul stew, Darryl Jones' snappy bass guitar stirring the meat and potatoes.

CHILDREN'S CRUSADE

One of the gems from 'Blue Turtles' that floats on a rhapsodic piano theme gently set in place by Kenny Kirkland. Sting's lyrics, full of sad irony, are rendered ever more effective by his understated treatment. Marsalis launches into a soprano sax solo of extraordinary power and intensity, spurred on by Hakim's drums that increase in power and fury without once losing control.

DOWN SO LONG

Rhythm and blues rule. Marsalis gets into Junior Walker mode and the drums and bass spoil for a fight. Sting must have felt like he was being pushed along by giants as he cajoles Kenny Kirkland to play a guitar-like keyboard solo. All clever stuff. Joked Sting in his original notes to the CD release: "Part of my campaign to convince the band that the blues is a music form indigenous to the coal-fields of Northern England – somehow I don't think they believe me."

TEA IN THE SAHARA

The last cut on 'Synchronicity', this moody piece was apparently Branford Marsalis' favourite Police track. This version was recorded in Arnhem, Holland and fades out, creating a sense of anti-climax after the excitement of 'Down So Long.'

Sting

..NOTHING LIKE THE SUN

NOTHING LIKE THE SUN

(ORIGINAL UK RELEASE A&M CDA 6402 OCTOBER 1987)

Sting's second studio album was recorded at AIR Studios, Montserrat, scene of previous Police efforts. It was produced by Neil Dorfsman and Sting, with Hugh Padgham brought in at the mixing stage. The album has a much sharper, cleaner sound than either 'Turtles' or 'Bring On The Night', and there is greater use of guitar.

Sting retained the services of some of his touring musicians, including Kenny Kirkland on keyboards and Branford Marsalis on saxophone. Manu Katchè came in on drums, while there was a plethora of guest guitarists. Andy Summers appeared on 'Lazarus Heart,' and 'Be Still My Beating Heart'. Mark Knopfler of Dire Straits, and Eric Clapton both played guitar on 'They Dance Alone', and Sting added his own guitar tracks and bass lines. Once again all the songs were written by Sting except for Jimi Hendrix's famed 'Little Wing'.

THE LAZARUS HEART

A strangely affecting song, with complex lyrics that Sting scans with a skill that non-singers perhaps take for granted. Sting muses on why tradition locates our emotional centre at the heart and not in the brain. The broken heart is one of the most prevalent images in pop music and Sting considers these aspects in a song he based on a vivid nightmare. The result is not dissimilar in mood to Jon Anderson's Yes hit 'Owner Of A Lonely Heart'.

BE STILL MY BEATING HEART

Hearts return again as Sting wrestles with the unbidden emotions that assail a man aroused by passion. "Be still my beating heart or I'll be taken for a fool," he warns. "It's not healthy to run at this pace, the blood runs so red to my face." There is only one cure for this problem. A cold shower and a slap. Few would dare

administer the latter at this stage in the composer's mega-successful career. The bass beats with a suitably throbbing pulse while the hi-hats click like a pace maker. Released as a single, this moody piece got to Number 15 in the US *Billboard* chart.

ENGLISHMAN IN NEW YORK

Calmly witty, lyrics set to a jaunty rhythm with what sounds suspiciously like a Rolf Harris' wobble board, enliven this curiosity which breaks into a most un-English swing time jazz solo. A rather silly poster of Sting bowing archly like a poltroon, which broke out in a rash all over New York City when it was released as a single, caused considerable embarrassment to all English visitors. The Americans weren't too impressed either as the single stalled at Number 84 in the US charts. "It takes a man to suffer ignorance and smile – be yourself no matter what they say," affirmed Sting. Alas it didn't do very well in the UK. So much for the influence of Quentin Crisp.

HISTORY WILL
TEACH US NOTHING

A dismal view of history teaching. It's true the same mistakes are repeated but usually by people who don't study history or much else for that matter. However Sting is adamant and warns: "If God is dead and an actor plays His part, his words of fear will find their way to a place in your heart. Without the voice of reason every faith is its own curse." How true.

A cool groove, and a terse, clipped reading of the lyrics nag away at the consciousness, making this one of the album's more insidious and intriguing performances. A rather unnecessary reggae interlude breaks the tension, but as Sting reminds us: "Sooner or later we learn to throw the past away." Wise words mate.

THEY DANCE ALONE
(GUECA SOLO)

A dramatic introduction full of slippery snare drum rolls paves the way for one of Sting's more than usually brilliant vocal performances. Sting is in sombre mood as he converts the humble pop song into a powerful political tool. His ghostly polemic points the figure at the leader of that South American country guilty of murdering and torturing its own people and whose victims are known as The Disappeared. Sting asks "Why are these women here dancing on their own? Why is there sadness in their eyes?" The answer is they're dancing with the missing… "They're dancing with the dead." Few artists have the courage to be so direct, as Sting calmly poses the question: "Hey Mr. Pinochet, you've sown a bitter crop. It's foreign money that supports you. One day the money's going to stop. No wages for your torturers, no budget for your guns. Can you think of your own mother dancing with her invisible son."

Sting uses his capacity for reaching a mass audience to convey an important message. The composer was influenced by his meetings with former political prisoners and victims of torture during the 1986 Amnesty Tour. "It's one thing to read about torture, but to speak to a victim brings you a step closer to the reality that is so frighteningly pervasive," he said. The 'Gueca' he explained was a traditional Chilean courting dance. 'The Gueca Solo' – or dance alone – is performed by the wives, daughters and mothers of the 'disappeared.' Said Sting: "It is a symbolic gesture of protest and grief in a country where democracy doesn't need to be 'defended' so much as exercised." The song won an Ivor Novello award for Best Song in April 1989.

FRAGILE

As fragile as fragile is. Sting ponders on the futility of violence, and offers a poet's plea for an end to killing, inspired by the heightened conflict between warring political and criminal gangs that plague the world with deadly consequences.

WE'LL BE TOGETHER

A funky dance work-out, simple and intended for pure enjoyment after the heavy moods created by 'They Dance Alone' and 'Fragile.'

The great American public liked this more than 'Englishman In New York', and the discotheques rumbled to a predictable beat as the single rocketed up to Number 7 in the *Billboard* chart in October 1987. Warbles

Sting: "All I want to be is dancing here with you in my arms." Not a bad plan at that. Rock on you jive ass mother.

STRAIGHT TO MY HEART

Tricky Latin rhythms break up the flow as Sting swings and sways lightly through a chirpy song of love and marriage. "Come into my door, you'll never have to sweep the floor," he advises his loved one, which means either he has become an enlightened New Man or invested in a new Hoover.

ROCK STEADY

A nicely executed jive version of the story of Noah's Ark. Sting creates a super cool and amusing narrative. Wordy but fun.

SISTER MOON

Not a million miles from 'Summertime', but a singularly groovy and sensuous confection that is rendered more beautiful by the lush keyboard chords and haunting soprano sax. This is Sting reaching into Gershwin territory and unleashing some of the most sophisticated music of his career. A far cry from punk rock. Sting described it as: "A song for lunatics everywhere, for all of those whose sanity is dependent on the phases of the moon."

LITTLE WING

A tender hearted rendition of Jimi Hendrix's classic song, in which Sting opens up and fully exploits the nuances of Jimi's lyrics. A fine guitar solo from Hiram Bullock provides an unexpected highlight, while the Gil Evans orchestra adds a low key presence. This was the result of a meeting between Sting and Evans one night at Ronnie Scott's Club, in London. "He'd been a hero of mine since I was fifteen. He reminded me of one of those wise elders from *Star Trek* who are the sole survivors of a planet after some holocaust, the sole guardians of all the knowledge of their race." The two got on so well that a couple of years later Sting sang 'Little Wing' with Gil's band at Sweet Basil's Club in Greenwich Village. Sting's other reason for performing the song was that The Jimi Hendrix Experience was one of the first bands he ever saw, at the Club A Go-Go in Newcastle.

THE SECRET MARRIAGE

Adapted from a melody by Hans Eisler, a colleague of playwright Bertold Brecht, who fled Nazi Germany to live in America. Sting reports that the Nazis… "hounded him for the rest of his life in various disguises." The song celebrates the sort of bonding that requires no church service or company contract. Says Sting, somewhat mysteriously: "The secret marriage vow is never spoken, the secret marriage never can be broken." A gentle acoustic piano and double bass accompaniment gives a classical flavour to the piece that makes it all the more moving.

Pregnant pauses and a suspended final note must have led to much respectful coughing and nervous shuffling in the playback suite on its first airing.

Sting *The Soul Cages*

THE SOUL CAGES

(ORIGINAL UK RELEASE A&M CD 396 405 2, JANUARY 1991)

At this point in his career Sting had become rather overburdened with responsibilities and woes to the point where this good natured, sensitive and witty man began to be perceived as "an embarrassing, pretentious bore" (*The Sunday Times*, March 1993). He stood accused of do-gooding for Amnesty, touring the world's chat shows with a Kayapo Indian chief, and then writing 'Soul Cages,' an album about his father's death from cancer. It was understandable that Sting would want to express his feelings on subjects that should concern any intelligent man, but this album was perhaps one sack of woe too many for the British public to endure.

Eventually the album sold as well as his previous works, except in the UK where the subject matter of death from cancer was not regarded as suitable fare for light entertainment. Sting forewarned that it was an introspective album and that he had gone through considerable pain in writing the lyrics. His manager Miles Copeland said later: "That was a big mistake, and we couldn't correct it. If he hadn't said it was 'introspective' it would have been better received because there are actually a lot of up songs on there."

Despite these prognostications of gloom, 'Soul Cages' went straight to the Number One slot in the UK album charts in February, 1991 and was at Number Two in the US Top Ten hit in the States in February, 1991. Among the singles released from the album 'All This Time' was a Top Ten hit.

Recording took place in France and Italy, utilising a new Q Sound technique to give a three dimensional clarity. Sting worked once again with Manu Katché on drums, and with old friends Branford Marsalis and Kenny Kirkland. He had claimed he was suffering from writers' block before he could contemplate a follow up to 'Nothing Like The Sun'. It was therefore tragic that the source of inspiration that compelled

him to write should be the death of his father, which of necessity instilled a mournful flavour into much of the resultant work.

ISLAND OF SOULS

A serious song that with the best will in the world can only be described as exceedingly dull. However, the lyrics are lovingly constructed, with Sting's natural gift for creating emotion-charged couplets that peer into the souls of the deprived and exploited as they seek some glimmer of hope and salvation. The tale of Billy the riveter's son, "born within sight of the shipyard" is pierced by a suggestion of Northumbrian pipes wailing a bitter lament. As the performance develops the sails of the good ship 'Eleanor Rigby' are spied off shore. Without a bluff Scouser at the wheel bringing a touch of salty wit to enliven the voyage, this sluggish barge drags at anchor against a rip tide of indifference.

ALL THIS TIME

A brighter beat prevails as Manu Katchè springs in one bound from his snare drum to kick some life into the session. The lyrics are full of allusions to the Tyne river and fog. "If I had my way I'd take a boat from the river and I'd bury the old man… at sea" sings Sting over a flowing rhythm. Van Morrison might well have found this a pleasant enough song to cover - if he had a mind.

MAD ABOUT YOU

"Though all my kingdoms turn to sand and fall into the sea, I'm mad about you…" Here our poet compares the works of mankind – vulnerable, liable to decay and collapse – to the power of love. Ah, but love can turn to dust, if not watered with the tears of compassion.

JEREMIAH BLUES
(Part 1)

"Something wicked this way comes…" Shakespeare and Ray Bradbury – and now Sting – slip in a line that just leaps off the page and out of the speakers. A dose of bluesy paranoia that brings a much needed sense of urgency and grooviness. Nice guitar solo and nifty drumming. Pity they didn't record Part 11.

WHY SHOULD I CRY FOR YOU?

A question that can be answered only by the composer. A delicate soliloquy that requires much tasteful clicking from the drummer and swirling chords that push the sad young mariner far out to sea, there to drift for the remainder of his days, wrapped in contemplation. At least and at last, he assures the dear departed that: "I loved you in my fashion."

SAINT AGNES AND THE BURNING TRAIN

An instrumental interlude. Classical guitars dance and the world is put to rights.

THE WILD WILD SEA

A rather long-drawn-out saga, best heard while lying on the floor with a glass of brandy, and a cigar, there to ponder the symbolism. Sting embarks on life's voyage aboard a ship captained by his father and the sea salt tears flow amidst the winds of fate. Actually it's not so bad, if you happen to have a pulse rate lower than the average sloth.

THE SOUL CAGES

Just when you think Sting is going to collapse into a heap of lifeless sorrows, he revives his spirits somewhat with a sturdy thumping beat, but the message is the same, a series of allegories concerning the grim fate of working folk Up North…

"These are the souls of the broken factories these are the souls of a broken town…" he proclaims mournfully, with only an angry guitar riff for solace.

WHEN THE ANGELS FALL

So slow and boring it must have sent the drummer in search of oxygen to keep awake. Sting intones the anguished confessional lyrics with a dreary lack of passion. A far cry from Ziggy Elman's 'When The Angels Sing', a much more cheery prospect. The final bars drag out like lead weights being hauled up a hill. As an exercise in wrist slashing torment it certainly works well.

TEN SUMMONER'S TALES

(ORIGINAL UK RELEASE A&M CD 540075-2, MARCH 1993)

'**S**oul Cages' had been a big hit as befits a major star of Sting's calibre, but it left an uneasy feeling that the cheery singer of yesteryear had become a self-obsessed gloom and doom monger. This was a far cry from the real Sting and he set about repairing the damage by lightening the load, flinging off the burdens of the world that seemed to have become attached to his shoulders with ropes, and making an album of songs that were lighter and less introspective. There was humour and joy in his music once more and the world sighed a deep sigh of relief, doffed their caps and muttered amongst themselves that Sting was back – with a great record.

The title 'Ten Summoner's Tales' was inspired by Sting's love of Chaucer and the *Canterbury Tales*, which he read at school. The origin of his real surname 'Sumner' was related to the 'Summoners' bailiffs who in Chaucer's day extracted fines from those who wouldn't go to court.

The new album was produced by Hugh Padgham and Sting and recorded at Lake House, a Jacobean mansion in Wiltshire. The band included Dominic Miller (guitar), Vinnie Colaiuta (drums), David Sancious (keyboards), and Sting on bass, harmonica and saxophone. This team was augmented by sundry brass and string players and even Larry Adler, the famed harmonica player, made a guest appearance.

The 'Tales' were greeted with acclaim by critics who had previously chastised him for 'Nothing Like The Sun', and 'Soul Cages'. The CD was more accessible, had catchy tunes, and boasted some of Sting's finest songs. He told critic Paul Colbert: "The intention was to get out of the cycle of traumatic soul searching and confessional records, pulling your soul apart every time. I thought 'What am I – a songwriter or a psychoanalyst?'" After a heavy touring schedule Sting decided to write

some songs "just to amuse myself". This time he avoided writing about himself and his innermost thoughts and set out to entertain, choosing as his target audience, the band and his family. If the outside world liked it too – well that was a bonus. There were even some jokes – musical and lyrical. The world agreed, it was good to see that Sting had his sense of humour and proportion back.

PROLOGUE (IF I EVER LOSE MY FAITH IN YOU)

A superb song and an instant classic. Sung with a moving simplicity this packs more emotion and heartfelt passion than all the overwrought self-analysis of the previous few years. Sting tells how he has lost faith in scientists, politicians, even TV commentators, but assures a loved one that if he ever loses faith in her... well there'd be nothing left to do. Clever use of harmonica adds a human touch to the clipped precision of the beat.

LOVE IS STRONGER THAN JUSTICE (THE MAGNIFICENT SEVEN)

Vinnie Colaiuta, revered by his fellow drummers, emerged as one of the finest players of the Nineties, and here his mixture of loose limbed funk and machine tooled accuracy, prods Sting into one of his funkiest work-outs. There is even a touch of country music in the release. Are you sure Sting done it this way?

FIELDS OF GOLD

Not content with unleashing 'If I Ever Lose My Faith In You', Sting raises his shield and sword, to flaunt the banner of another magnificent song, delivered with a gentle sense of peace and poetry. This has the timeless appeal of a popular hymn and the surging strings and guitars add to the feeling of warmth and humanity.

HEAVY CLOUD NO RAIN

Pure funk, with the world's greatest rhythm section kicking up a groove that sees some of Sting's wittiest vocal games. He tells the endless tale of the prophets, astrologers and weather men who can't always tell which way the wind will blow.

SHE'S TOO GOOD FOR ME

If Sting was writing to entertain his band as well as the public, he certainly gave them something to get their teeth into with this rocking raver, with its unexpected time and mood changes and zappy ending. Sting imagines the super critical girlfriend who don't like nuthin' 'bout him. "She don't like the books I read... she don't like the way I feed, she don't want to save my life, she don't want to be my wife" he groans – with a smile.

SEVEN DAYS

A powerful and carefully constructed pop song, full of imaginative touches in a wide screen, panoramic arrangement rich in orchestral overtones. It sounds not unlike an overture from a Broadway musical of the Forties. Sting ponders over his love's ultimatum. It's him or a Neanderthal giant who must compete for her favours. While there is no competition in terms of IQ, says Sting wryly: "We won't be playing Scrabble for her hand I fear."

SAINT AUGUSTINE IN HELL

More blues, with a howling Hammond organ as our leader pours irony and scorn upon those who would be his judges and contemplates the temptations of the flesh. Jokes there are a-plenty and we are reliably informed that among the denizens of hell are high court judges, cardinals, archbishops, accountants and music critics.

IT'S PROBABLY ME

A thoughtful, pensive song contemplating who would turn out to be a true friend in an hour of need. "I hate to say it, but it's probably me." Muted trumpet adds to the mood of empty cocktail bars, deserted city streets and lost souls. Who me?

EVERYBODY LAUGHED BUT YOU

More sophisticated finely tuned lyrics that would not have disgraced Noël Coward. Friends lost *en route* to success and their place at the top of the tree are mourned or remembered, leaving just one friend, the one who always remained loyal and true.

SHAPE OF MY HEART

An immensely sad ballad, made even more gut wrenching by the use of Spanish acoustic guitar and Larry Adler's masterful harmonica. Both Sting and pop music grew up to reach a higher plane with this flawless gem that sustains its sentiments without ever sinking into mere sentimentality.

SOMETHING THE BOY SAID

Said the boy... "you'll never see our faces again." Sting's words flow with a story teller's art, gripping, haunting and not revealing their full message until the dénouement. "We would never have marched so far to be food for a crow," the troops tell the Captain whose son had warned them of the bloody fate that lay in store. The drums tick with a clockwork regularity as the harmonica – the trench warfare soldier's favourite instrument – returns to heighten the air of foreboding.

EPILOGUE

(NOTHIN 'BOUT ME)

For many this is the favourite song on a highly regarded album that makes a wonderfully warm, amusing, and highly pertinent postscript to Sting's career thus far. All pain is banished and youthful indiscretions forgotten. Here he intones, with a twinkle in the eye and a chuckle in his larynx: "Check my facts, check if I paid my income tax, pore over everything in my C.V. but you'll still know nothing 'bout me." He has a strong point to make. In the final analysis, as the band sing along in Glenn Miller fashion, and the relentless rising bass line takes the Epilogue to its ecstatic, sarcastic conclusion, you have to admit – Sting wins on all counts.

INDEX

POLICE

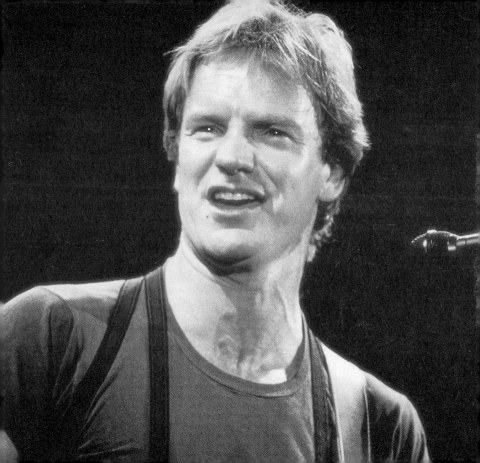

STING